Saddam's Iraq

Face-Off in the Gulf

REUTERS

Published by **Prentice Hall**

ISBN 0-13-141153-5

9 780131 411531

Library of Congress Cataloging-in-Publication Data

A CIP catalog record for this book can be obtained from the Library of Congress

Publisher: Tim Moore
Executive editor: Jim Boyd
Director of production: Sophie Papanikolaou
Production supervisor: Patti Guerrieri
Marketing manager: John Pierce
Manufacturing manager: Alexis Heydt-Long

Editorial assistant: Linda Ramagnano
Cover design director: Jerry Votta
Cover designer: Anthony Gemmellaro
Art director: Gail Cocker-Bogusz
Interior design and layout: Meg Van Arsdale

Reuters
Executive editor: Stephen Jukes
Coordinating editor: Peter Millership
Commercial manager: Alisa Bowen
Front cover art photographer: Jerry Lampen
Cover photo copyright © 2002 Reuters

In compiling this book, thanks go to many people. At Reuters, Doina Chiacu, David Cutler, Bernd Debusmann, Giles Elgood, Mikhail Evstafiev, Gary Hershorn, Nadim Ladki, Evelyn Leopold, Samia Nakhoul, Caroline Powell, Paul Scruton, Alexia Singh, Tim Langton, Mark Trevelyan, Mike Tyler, Patrick Worsnip, David Viggers and Mohammad Zargham.

© 2003 Reuters
Published by Pearson Education Inc.
Publishing as Reuters Prentice Hall
Upper Saddle River, NJ 07458

Prentice Hall books are widely used by corporations and government agencies for training, marketing and resale.

For information regarding corporate and government bulk discounts please contact: Corporate and Government Sales (800) 382-3419, or corpsales@pearsontechgroupl.com.

Printed in the United States of America

10 9 8 7 6 5 4 3 2 1

ISBN 0-13-141153-5

Pearson Education LTD.
Pearson Education Australia PTY, Limited
Pearson Education Singapore, Pte. Ltd.
Pearson Education North Asia Ltd.
Pearson Education Canada, Ltd.
Pearson Educación de Mexico, S.A. de C.V.
Pearson Education—Japan
Pearson Education Malaysia, Pte. Ltd.

Contents

Saddam's Iraq

Face-Off in the Gulf

Face-Off in the Gulf

Mark Trevelyan

"To assume this regime's good faith is to bet the lives of millions and the peace of the world in a reckless gamble. And this is a risk we must not take."

President George W. Bush
in an address to the United Nations,
September 12, 2002

"We are preparing for war as if war will break out in one hour, and we are psychologically ready for that."

Iraqi President Saddam Hussein,
November 3, 2002

The Case for War

The sense of expectation at United Nations headquarters was palpable. A year and a day after Arab suicide squads crashed hijacked airliners into the World Trade Center and the Pentagon, President George W. Bush was due to deliver a crucial speech that could open a fresh chapter in his war on terror. World leaders in his audience could find themselves "squirming in some of the seats," a senior administration official warned beforehand. Bush would be blunt.

At home and abroad, it had been an anxious few days. The anniversary of September 11 had revived traumatic memories and fears of fresh attacks on America. Vice President Dick Cheney was at a secret location. Heat-seeking anti-aircraft missiles were deployed around Washington in an operation codenamed Noble Eagle. A number of U.S. embassies around the world were closed for security reasons. Airlines slashed their schedules as passengers chose not to fly on September 11, fearing a spectacular new coup by the authors of the original attacks. Chief suspect Osama bin Laden and most of the top lieutenants in his al Qaeda network were believed to be still alive, scattered but elusive, and capable of posing a lethal threat.

But the U.S. president made no mention of bin Laden. In a speech of 2,700 words, he named al Qaeda just once. Instead, Bush devoted almost his entire address to warning the world of what he saw as the threat from one country: Saddam Hussein's Iraq. He painted a detailed picture of a brutal and devious dictator who had defied the international community for 12 years, breaking his

Saddam Hussein presides over what appeared to be the biggest military parade in Baghdad since the 1991 Gulf War, greeting the massed ranks with gunfire, December 31, 2000. REUTERS

promises and defying U.N. resolutions aimed at forcing him to disarm. Saddam, said Bush, was relentlessly pursuing weapons of mass destruction.

"The first time we may be completely certain he has nuclear weapons is when, God forbid, he uses one," Bush said. He outlined a nightmare scenario—"our greatest fear"—in which an "outlaw regime" like Saddam's might supply doomsday weapons to a terrorist group.

The emphasis on Saddam came as no surprise for those who tracked U.S. policy. Bush and leading figures in his administration had inexorably turned their sights on Iraq as part of a gradual but critically important shift in U.S. security doctrine since September 11, 2001. It was his conscious choice to restore Iraq to the very top of the U.S. agenda and actively seek to bring about "regime change," a U.S. policy first stated under his predecessor Bill Clinton. By a quirk of history, he found himself in a position to complete the unfinished business of his father, President George Bush senior, who routed Saddam's forces in the 1991 Gulf War but left the Iraqi leader in power.

As the younger Bush built up pressure on Saddam, underpinned by the threat of U.S.-led military action, there were parallels with, but also sharp differences from the build-up to his father's war. In 1991, the justification under international law was clear, and the arguments were easier to sell to the Arab world and the wider international community. War had to be fought to reverse an act of aggression— Iraq's invasion of Kuwait—and drive the occupying troops out.

More than a decade later, Washington's case is built around the alleged potential for future Iraqi aggression and the argument that such threats must be crushed before they materialize. Opponents see this as morally flawed, in breach of international law and fraught with the danger of destabilizing the whole of the Middle East. Some, including Iraq itself, say America's real agenda is to gain control over Iraq's vast oil reserves.

But Bush, driven by the imperatives of his war on terror, has invested much of his personal credibility in the campaign to remove Saddam. If he is determined to go ahead, there is little to stop him. In the post-Cold War world, the United States enjoys unquestioned military pre-eminence. And since the attacks of September 11, 2001, that domination has been underpinned by a sharper sense of purpose and the willingness to go it alone, when required, to pursue U.S. security interests anywhere in the world.

Many of the risks confronting Bush are the same as those his father chose not to run in 1991—U.S. military and Iraqi civilian casualties; massive refugee flows; civil war in Iraq, with its volatile ethnic and religious mix; the export of instability to Turkey, Syria, Iran and beyond; the difficulty of installing a democratic government in Baghdad and the prospect of a costly and open-ended U.S. commitment, both military and financial, to shore it up. Other dangers are potentially even greater now than then. With Arabs already seething over U.S. backing for Israel in its two-year struggle against a Palestinian uprising, war on Iraq could fuel anti-American rage across the region of the very kind that inspired the September 11 attacks. Bush, some fear, could be playing right into bin Laden's hands.

If the U.S. president is prepared to run such risks, it may be because the dangers of failing to act, as he sees them, are even greater— but also because the potential rewards are enticing. If "regime change" works in Iraq, some analysts argue, the United States may not stop there. Saddam is not the only Arab leader that Bush wants to see gone. He has called already for the removal of Palestinian President Yasser Arafat, whom Israel accuses of failing to rein in suicide bombers, and urged Arafat's people to elect new leaders "not compromised by terror." Others could join Saddam and Arafat on that list. In a vision only hinted at by Bush, but explicitly outlined by some prominent U.S. conservatives, Iraq could be just the first step in a U.S.-led drive to re-engineer the Middle East along democratic, free-market lines and

Taken from the roof of the International Press Center in Baghdad, this picture shows Iraqi anti-aircraft guns firing at U.S. and British warplanes carrying out strikes on the city under Operation Desert Fox, December 19, 1998. REUTERS

remake a region whose vast oil wealth—of huge strategic importance to the United States—has been mainly exploited for the benefit of narrow elites.

"Saddam's replacement by a decent Iraqi regime would open the way to a far more stable and peaceful region," Pentagon adviser Richard Perle said in a British newspaper interview. "A democratic Iraq would be a powerful refutation of the patronizing view that Arabs are incapable of democracy."

The stakes could not be higher. A quick, decisive war with Iraq could help vindicate the new, assertive American doctrine of pre-emptive military action and entrench it for decades to come. But if war drags on, Bush risks a wider conflagration that would not only doom his own presidency but could spread turmoil throughout the region and provoke more attacks by extremists, the very opposite of what he is trying to achieve.

The Bush Doctrine

In truth, Iraq has never been off the U.S. agenda since the 1991 Gulf War. But for the ensuing decade, Washington was content for the most part to keep Saddam "in his box"—tying him down with sanctions and isolating him as an international pariah.

Two things changed that. The first was the arrival of a Republican administration with unfinished business with Iraq and the second was September 11. When the Arab hijackers turned commercial airliners into missiles and smashed them into New York's World Trade Center and the Pentagon, they struck at the nerve centers of U.S. financial, political and military power. Another plane which could have caused further chaos crashed in a field in Pennsylvania after passengers apparently rushed the hijackers.

Americans had suffered deadly attacks abroad—in the Middle East and East Africa, for example—but never before had they sustained such a devastating blow on mainland U.S. soil. America's view of the world was transformed, and so too was the Bush presidency. A leader who had taken power with an overwhelmingly domestic agenda was forced to rededicate his presidency to one central international mission, the war on terror. The overriding goal was the pursuit of bin Laden and al Qaeda. America would act alongside allies where it could, but alone where needed. Relations with every country would be governed by the requirements of this war: "Either you are with us or you are with the terrorists," the president declared. Bush would root out enemies and threats to the United States, wherever they arose in the world. He began in Afghanistan, where the United States threw its weight behind the opposition Northern Alliance. The ruling Taliban, sponsors and hosts of al Qaeda, were quickly routed by the combination of U.S. air power and Northern Alliance forces on the ground.

A defining moment came with Bush's State of the Union speech in January 2002. The Taliban were vanquished, al Qaeda dispersed, and the bin Laden trail had gone cold. The name of Osama, the enemy whom Bush had denounced as the "evil one" and wanted "dead or alive," was mentioned increasingly rarely by U.S. officials. Where was the war on terror going from here?

Enter the "Axis of Evil." It was in this speech that Bush first coined that term and applied it to three countries—Iraq, Iran and North Korea—which he accused of developing weapons of mass destruction. At a

Iraqi women shout and cry in the village of Jassan after U.S. and British air strikes, August 18, 1999. The U.S. military's Southern Command said the raids took place after Iraqi anti-aircraft artillery fired at Western planes. REUTERS

stroke, Bush was widening the definition of the war on terror: the fight against weapons proliferation would now be a crucial part of the struggle. In a June 1, 2002, speech at West Point military academy, Bush developed his new doctrine further, stressing the need for pre-emptive military action where necessary to stop "terrorists and tyrants" from obtaining weapons of mass destruction. "If we wait for threats to fully materialize, we will have waited too long. We must take the battle to the enemy, disrupt his plans and confront the worst threats before they emerge."

The fullest expression of America's new security stance came in a strategy report released on September 20, 2002. Building on the West Point theme, the administration affirmed the need to defeat terrorism by "destroying the threat before it reaches our borders." It went further: moving away from traditional Cold War policies of containment and deterrence, the United States asserted its own military pre-eminence and the need to prevent its rivals from matching it.

"Our forces will be strong enough to dissuade potential adversaries from pursuing a military buildup in hopes of surpassing, or equaling, the power of the United States," the document said.

Many aspects of these new policies drew criticism. Opponents condemned the "Axis of Evil" as a distortion, implying an alliance between the three named countries that did not exist in reality. Rather like Bush's Wild West-style "dead or alive" rhetoric toward bin Laden, critics saw it as reflecting a naïve, simplistic view of a world divided between good guys and bad guys. To America's enemies and even some of its friends, the new U.S. strategy showed a worrying unilateralist, even imperialist, streak. But the switch reflected a strong sense among Americans that previous security mechanisms had failed and needed replacing. September 11 had exposed a need for new thinking. Increasingly it began to look as though Iraq would provide the first test of the Bush doctrine.

Why Iraq, Why Now?

Back in 1991, Saddam had promised an epic struggle, the Mother of All Battles, as the U.S.-led coalition assembled a massive army to drive him out of Kuwait. It turned out to be a grotesque mismatch. On January 17,

Post-Gulf War Chronology

1991

Feb 28   U.S. and allied forces cease fire.

Apr 7   The United States, Britain and France set up a "no-fly zone" north of the 36th parallel.

Apr 11   The United Nations declares formal Gulf War ceasefire.

Jun 9   The U.N. Special Commission (UNSCOM) starts chemical weapons inspections.

Jun 28   Iraqi soldiers fire shots into the air when U.N. inspectors try to photograph a speeding convoy carrying crates of nuclear-related material.

1993

Jun   U.S. warships fire 23 cruise missiles at Baghdad, destroying Iraqi intelligence service headquarters wing. Missiles kill six people. Attack ordered to avenge alleged Iraqi plot to kill former U.S. President George Bush.

1995

Jul 1   Iraq admits for the first time that it has biological weapons.

1996

Dec 10   The oil for food deal comes into effect, allowing Iraq to sell $2 billion worth of oil for six months to buy humanitarian supplies for its people.

1997

Oct 29   Iraq bars Americans from weapons teams.

1998

Aug 9   UNSCOM suspends inspections of new sites after Baghdad decides to halt cooperation with United Nations.

Nov 14/15 President Clinton halts two planned air strikes after Iraq offers to let inspections resume.

Dec 16 United Nations inspectors are withdrawn from Baghdad.

Dec 17 United States and Britain stage four days of air strikes at Iraqi factories, political, military and intelligence headquarters as punishment for not cooperating with inspectors.

2000

Mar 26 President Saddam Hussein meets outgoing U.N. relief coordinator Hans von Sponeck, the first time he has met an Iraqi-based U.N. official since the 1991 Gulf War.

2002

Jan 29 In a speech, President George W. Bush says Iran, Iraq and North Korea form an "axis of evil" developing weapons of mass destruction; all three reject the accusation the next day.

Sep 12 Bush challenges U.N. General Assembly to disarm Iraq or the United States would do it alone.

Sep 16 U.N. Secretary-General Kofi Annan receives a letter from the Iraqi authorities agreeing to allow the return of U.N. inspectors without conditions.

Oct Mohammed Aldouri, Iraq's ambassador to the United Nations, says that 1.7 million people have died as a result of U.N. sanctions.

Oct 12 An adviser to Saddam sends a letter to U.N. weapons inspectors saying Iraq is ready to remove all obstacles to a return of inspectors after nearly four years.

Nov 8 U.N. Security Council unanimously approves resolution directing Iraq to disarm or face "serious consequences" and giving inspectors new rights.

(continued)

Nov 13   Iraq accepts U.N. resolution in an angry letter to Annan.

Nov 18   Advance party of U.N. inspectors land in Baghdad for first time in four years.

U.S.-led forces began weeks of air and missile attacks. On February 24 they followed up with a ground offensive that lasted exactly 100 hours. With Iraqi forces fleeing in disarray, Bush senior called a halt to military operations from midnight Washington time on February 27, 1991. The Gulf War had ended in a crushing victory for the United States and its allies: less than seven months after invading Kuwait, Iraqi troops had been routed and expelled.

The United States could have gone further. In purely military terms, there was no question that it could have pursued the retreating Iraqis all the way to Baghdad. General Norman Schwarzkopf declared victory at a news conference, dubbed the "mother of all briefings," and said his forces could have overrun the country unopposed if that had been their intention.

But there were compelling political reasons to stop the war. President George Bush senior had painstakingly assembled a wide coalition—including traditional Arab foes such as Syria—for the express purpose of liberating Kuwait, not toppling Saddam. Ousting him would have gone far beyond the terms of United Nations resolutions. It would have meant higher U.S. casualties. There was no clear vision of who or what would replace him, and any successor government would have required substantial, costly and open-ended support, both military and financial. Not only did Bush call off the land war, but he declined to throw U.S. support behind the Kurds of

An Iraqi soldier gestures to weapons inspectors as they drive out of U.N. headquarters in Baghdad, November 23, 1998. REUTERS

northern Iraq or the Shias in the south, both of whom launched uprisings against Saddam almost as soon as the Gulf war was over. Successful revolts by either group would have carried unpredictable consequences and risks for both Iraq and its neighbors. Better for the United States to declare "mission accomplished" and withdraw its forces quickly from the region. In any case, many assumed Saddam was already fatally weakened and on the verge of being toppled. "We thought Saddam Hussein would leave power," Bush senior said in a speech in October 2002.

That assumption with hindsight proved at best naïve. Twelve years of sanctions failed to break Saddam. A U.N.-administered "oil for food" program allowed Iraq to export oil in order to buy essential goods, but glaring shortages of medicines caused indisputable suffering and handed a propaganda opportunity to the Iraqis, who blamed the sanctions for the deaths of 1.7 million people.

More than a decade after the war, Bush junior had personal as well as political motives for preoccupying himself with Saddam. In his U.N. speech, he alluded to Iraq's attempt to kill "a former American president" in a plot foiled by U.S. intelligence in Kuwait in 1993. On another occasion he spoke of the episode—and Saddam—in more personal terms: "After all, this is the guy who tried to kill my dad." Two other top figures in his administration had cause to see the Gulf War as unfinished business: Vice President Cheney had been defense secretary under Bush senior, while Secretary of State Colin Powell was the former chairman of the Joint Chiefs of Staff.

In the wake of September 11, Bush and his Republican team saw a new opportunity to go after Saddam and remove this thorn in their side. Buoyed by strong public support, heightened patriotism and a bipartisan political consensus, they spotted a chance to test and validate their new security doctrine. "Before September 11 there would really have been no chance whatsoever of mobilizing the American people or the Congress behind a unilateral attack on Iraq or indeed any kind of pre-emptive strike against Iraq. It would just have been politically out of the question," said Anatol Lieven of the Carnegie Endowment for International Peace in Washington. "They're trying to use the nationalist energy generated by September 11 to carry a war with Iraq."

Former U.N. arms inspector Scott Ritter avoids walking on a portrait of former President George Bush as he enters the al-Rashid hotel in Baghdad, July 29, 2000. Ritter arrived in Baghdad to film a documentary about weapons sites and the impact of U.N. sanctions. REUTERS

Domestic political considerations came into the equation. With an eye to his own re-election chances in 2004, the war on terror provided Bush with a unifying national cause, and he built up broad popular backing. He had fashioned it into the defining theme of his presidency, and opponents risked being branded unpatriotic or wimpish. Amid global and U.S. economic malaise, a prolonged stock-market downturn and a spate of corporate scandals, decisive leadership and defense of America's security interests were his strongest political asset.

Against this background, Bush began to set out before the American people and the world community a case for possible war against Iraq. Much of it was laid out in his U.N. speech on September 12, in which he declared: "Saddam Hussein's regime is a grave and gathering danger." It was reinforced by Britain's Prime Minister Tony Blair, Bush's closest ally, in a published dossier of evidence based partly on intelligence reports.

Chief among the Bush/Blair arguments were these: Saddam had a clear record of aggression against his neighbors, with attacks on Iran in 1980 and Kuwait in 1990. He had repressed his own people, even using deadly poison gas against Iraqi Kurds in 1988. He was determinedly pursuing chemical, biological and atomic weapons and could build a nuclear device within a year if he got hold of fissile material. He had broken every promise to the United Nations and prevented arms inspectors from pursuing their work. Saddam was a threat to the world and to the authority of the United Nations, which risked irrelevance if it failed to oppose him.

Going beyond the Blair dossier and London's more cautious line, Bush and administration officials frequently asserted links between Saddam and al Qaeda. "This is a man that we know has had connections with al Qaeda. This is a man who, in my judgment, would like to use al Qaeda as a forward army," the president declared. Secretary of Defense Donald Rumsfeld said in late September 2002 that senior al Qaeda leaders had been in Baghdad in the previous weeks. "We have what we believe to be credible information that Iraq and al Qaeda have discussed safe-haven opportunities in Iraq, reciprocal nonaggression discussions. We have what we consider to be credible evidence that al Qaeda have sought contacts in Iraq who could help them acquire weapons of mass-destruction capabilities."

This drumbeat from the administration appeared to yield results. By the following month, an opinion poll showed two-thirds of Americans, despite the absence of any "smoking gun," believed Saddam had a hand in the September 11 attacks.

The Case Against

Yet the administration was far from having things all its own way. Every strand of its case for war was scrutinized by enemies and allies alike and minutely examined in the media. Both Czech President Vaclav Havel and the CIA discredited the strongest circumstantial link between Iraq and al Qaeda—a reported meeting in Prague in April 2001 between September 11 hijack leader Mohammed Atta and an Iraqi intelligence official. Many commentators trashed the notion of

Weapons inspectors prepare a site in Iraq for the destruction of rockets containing the chemical nerve agent sarin, February 16, 1998. REUTERS

U.N. Inspectors:
The Search for Weapons of Mass Destruction

Evelyn Leopold

"At one level, major world leaders have major world weapons, or to put it more colloquially, big boys have big toys."

Jerrold Post
professor of political psychology at
George Washington University

Scuds, super guns, calutrons, anthrax, botulinum toxin, sulphur mustard, nitrogen mustard, sarin nerve agents, VX nerve agents. It was supposed to take only 45 days in 1991 to get rid of them all, but more than a decade later no one is sure what is left.

At the end of the 1991 Gulf War, the United States and others believed that President Saddam Hussein would act as the leader of a defeated nation and give up weapons of mass destruction. Otherwise he would continue to lose $25 million a day in oil revenues, the heart of sweeping U.N. sanctions.

To this end, the U.N. Security Council in April 1991 adopted a complex 3,900-word cease-fire resolution, No. 687, which, in effect, dictated Iraq's surrender. The measure set up the world's most intrusive inspection system to rid Iraq of ballistic missiles and nuclear, chemical and biological weapons as a condition for lifting the embargo on oil.

The first inspection unit, known as the U.N. Special Commission or UNSCOM, was created with Rolf Ekeus, a Swedish diplomat and disarmament expert, as its executive chairman. When Ekeus walked into his office in April 1991, he had a desk, a chair and a secretary, Olivia Platon, then on loan from the U.N. Center for Disarmament.

By the time Ekeus handed UNSCOM over to Australian Richard Butler in July 1997, he had hundreds of inspectors, a headquarters staff, the use of satellites, helicopters, cameras, equipment to measure air, water and soil, a testing facility in Baghdad and intelligence reports from governments.

By 1998 the inspectors had accounted for or destroyed equipment and materials that could be used to make an atomic bomb, 817 of 819 Scud missiles,

39,000 chemical munitions and more than 3,000 tons of agents and precursors. But unaccounted for were 500 mustard-gas shells, 150 aerial bombs, 17 tons of complex growth media that could be used to nourish biological agents, and 200 tons of chemicals for the nerve agent VX.

In hindsight, the carrot-and-stick approach was doomed almost from the start. Saddam neither admitted defeat nor wanted to be portrayed as "disarmed." Weapons inspectors blowing up factories or driving up to government ministries unannounced were an unexpected affront to what Iraqi officials called their "sovereignty, security and independence."

The incentive of lifting the oil sanctions also disappeared quickly. The first President George Bush, facing criticism for leaving Saddam in office after the Gulf War, said as early as May 1991 that he did not want to lift sanctions "as long as Saddam Hussein is in power," a contradiction of resolution 687.

The scene was set. Iraq at first "was merely offering up its obsolete and dangerous stock for UNSCOM to destroy, and keeping back its more modern

A building inside one of Baghdad's presidential palace compounds, an area off limits to United Nations weapons inspectors at the time, was photographed on a media trip organized by Iraqi Deputy Prime Minister Tareq Aziz, December 19, 1997. REUTERS

(continued)

and useful weapons," wrote Tim Trevan, UNSCOM's press spokesman in *Saddam's Secrets: The Hunt for Iraq's Hidden Weapons.*

In June 1991 David Kay, an inspector from the International Atomic Energy Agency, carried out the first surprise survey at the Fallujah camp, northwest of Baghdad. His group was photographing Iraqis loading into trucks bomb-making equipment, called calutrons, an antique technology used to separate atomic weapons-grade material. To stop the inspectors from getting closer, soldiers fired shots into the air.

Three months later Kay and his team were pinned down in a parking lot for days for refusing to give back documents, which in subsequent years were either handed over to UNSCOM by the truckload or refused entirely. Ekeus was called a "liar" by Iraqi officials, and inspectors Nikita Smidovich of Russia and Scott Ritter of the United States were referred to as "cowboys."

To bring the inspections back on track, the United States periodically threatened war, several times in 1998, dubbed the "year of the palaces." Butler in December 1997 was unable to gain access to Saddam's "palaces"—in reality eight huge presidential sites with more than 1,000 buildings. The inspectors hoped to find documents that would unravel the decision-making process by which Iraq had concealed a secret arsenal.

U.N. Secretary-General Kofi Annan, in an effort to avoid war, struck a deal that required inspectors to be accompanied by foreign diplomats. American Charles Duelfer, who led a 75-car caravan on the only inspection of the compounds, said no one learned anything. "The Iraqis had plenty of time to prepare. You couldn't get a cleaning service in Washington that was that good," he said.

Iraq evidently had decided that without a definitive promise to lift sanctions, it would make its case around the world against intrusive inspections. Although Baghdad now was allowed to sell unlimited amounts of oil, its imports of goods were controlled by the United Nations, which micromanaged the Iraqi economy under the "oil-for-food" program.

For many countries, fatigue and opposition to the sanctions had set in. Even if Saddam had built some luxury homes, the population was clearly suffering under the embargoes, especially children. The U.N. Security Council was bitterly divided, with Russia, France and others calling for steps toward lifting sanctions.

UNSCOM, in effect, was put on trial, its status diminished, its methods questioned. In December 1998, Butler gave another negative report on Iraqi cooperation. He then withdrew the inspectors, hours before the United States and Britain launched Operation Desert Fox, four days of relentless aerial bombardment of Iraqi facilities.

It was the end of inspections and, within a year, the end of UNSCOM itself.

The commission was harshly criticized by Russia and other council members, particularly after U.S. officials in 1999 openly admitted they had placed spies among the inspectors. In December 1999, after months of haggling, a divided Security Council created a new unit, the U.N. Monitoring, Verification and Inspection Commission. Hans Blix, the retired Swedish director of the International Atomic Energy Agency, became its executive chairman.

But Iraq had had enough. It refused to allow the weapons inspectors to return unconditionally until mid-2002, again under the threat of a full-scale U.S. invasion, this time aimed at toppling Saddam himself. Inspections were in vogue again. The inspectors, once accused of provoking a war, were now seen as the only means to prevent or delay Washington from launching a military strike.

a link between the militant Islamist Osama bin Laden and the militant secularist Saddam Hussein. French President Jacques Chirac said no direct connection had been established—or at least made public—between Iraq and al Qaeda. *The New York Times*, in an editorial, accused the Bush administration of making "confused and scattered assertions about Iraq" and urged it to lay out a clear and unambiguous case.

Few of Bush's critics around the world disputed his portrait of Saddam Hussein as a tyrant, but many took issue with his depiction of the threat from Baghdad. His case for war rested largely on assertions of an Iraqi weapons buildup that were emphatically denied by Baghdad and could not be proved or disproved in the absence of arms inspections.

Yet when Iraq offered to welcome back weapons teams without pre-conditions, Washington dismissed it as a ruse and refused to send them back without a tough new U.N. resolution underpinned by the threat of force. "In short, the administration really does not know whether there is a clear and imminent threat from Iraq, cannot prove that one exists, and resists proposals for finding out because the answer might undermine its plans for war," wrote Paul W. Schroeder, political science professor at the University of Illinois.

Iraqi employees walk by a wall of a former uranium extraction plant that was destroyed in 1991 by U.S. warplanes at al Qaim, Anbar province, September 2, 2002. REUTERS

Why is Saddam in 2002 more dangerous, and more of a threat to the United States, than Saddam in 1991 or at any time in between? If he does indeed possess weapons of mass destruction, is there really any hard evidence he plans to use them against his enemies and risk the massive Israeli or U.S. retribution that would certainly follow? Why does possession of such arms—the same weapons already at the disposal of the United States, its allies and a number of neutral countries—constitute grounds for war? The implication of this, Schroeder argued in an essay, was that there was one law for the United States and its friends and another for everyone else. "It is Orwellian: all states are equal, but some, especially the United States, are vastly more equal than others. There is no state, allied, friendly, neutral, or hostile, that will not note this implication, and fear it."

Sure enough, prominent U.S. allies were among those most vocal in questioning Bush's intentions. Germany's Gerhard Schroeder, fighting the closest of election campaigns, saw votes to be won from declaring he would never lead the country into a military "adventure" against Iraq. Politically, he made the right calculation, squeezing his way to a narrow victory at the cost of severely damaging ties with Washington. And as the Iraqi issue was thrashed out in the United Nations, it was two more U.S. allies, France and Russia, which led opposition to any resolution containing "automatic triggers" for war against Saddam. They finally settled for a resolution, passed unanimously on November 8, which gave Baghdad a "final opportunity" to comply with U.N. disarmament demands. Iraq agreed to accept it on November 13.

Before the 1991 Gulf War, the Security Council had authorized "all necessary means" to reverse the Iraqi invasion of Kuwait. This time

An Iraqi boy sits between a soldier and a woman holding up a portrait of the Iraqi leader at a pro-Saddam demonstration outside U.N. headquarters in Baghdad, February 24, 1998. REUTERS

around the situation was murkier and the resolution was less clear-cut. In deference to the French and Russians, it called for a meeting of the Council to consider any Iraqi breaches reported by arms inspectors. On the other hand, it did not require any fresh Council vote on the consequences of such breaches, and the United States made clear that any false step would lead to war. "The U.N. can meet and discuss, but we don't need their permission," White House Chief of Staff Andrew Card said.

Risks of War

As well as opposing on principles, Bush's critics mustered an array of practical arguments against attacking Saddam. Not only, they contended, was he resorting to a crude bullying doctrine which amounted to "might is right." He risked setting the whole of the Middle East alight and pouring fresh fuel on the fire of Islamic militancy, within and beyond the region.

Unhelpfully for Bush, it was his own Central Intelligence Agency that highlighted the risk that U.S. military action to oust Saddam and rid Iraq of weapons of mass destruction would actually increase the chance of his using such weapons. In a letter released in October 2002, the agency said the probability of Saddam's attacking the United States without provocation in the foreseeable future was "very low." But if attacked, the likelihood that he would respond with chemical or biological weapons was "pretty high."

"Baghdad for now appears to be drawing a line short of conducting terrorist attacks with conventional or CBW (chemical and biological weapons) against the United States," the agency said. "Should Saddam conclude that a U.S.-led attack could no longer be deterred, he probably would become much less constrained in adopting terrorist actions."

In a Reuters poll of global defense analysts in October 2002, 10 out of 22 respondents said Saddam was likely or very likely to use weapons of mass destruction against the United States or its allies in a conflict. Fourteen saw a significant or moderate risk that conflict could spread to other oil-producing countries in the region through external attack or internal revolt. And most saw a significant or very significant risk of an Iraqi conflict provoking terror attacks on the United States or its allies.

Among the most vociferous critics of the U.S. military buildup were the regional players themselves. Egypt's Amr Moussa, head of the Arab League, said war would "open the gates of hell" in the Middle East. Syria's President Bashar al-Assad, in a rare interview, told Reuters: "Nobody should go to war because he does or doesn't like this or that country. You cannot change the regime without killing millions of Iraqis."

Six countries share borders with Iraq: Kuwait, Jordan, Turkey, Syria, Iran and Saudi Arabia. All had reasons to fear the fallout from a U.S. invasion of Iraq, though none had cause to mourn Saddam's passing.

Kuwait, invaded by Saddam in 1990, could find itself in the firing line again if the CIA scenario came to pass and the cornered Iraqi leader, with nothing left to lose, chose to unleash on his regional enemies whatever chemical and biological weapons he might possess.

Jordan's young King Abdullah, on the throne only since 1999, was unlikely to anger the United States by sympathizing with Saddam as his father King Hussein had done in 1991. But he risked the anger of his own people, anti-American demonstrations on the streets and damage to his country's vulnerable economy, overdependent on trade with Baghdad and supplies of cheap Iraqi oil.

Turkey, Syria and Iran, all with substantial Kurdish minorities, had special reason to fear the fragmentation of Iraq along ethnic and religious lines. With its mixture of Kurds in the north, majority Shias in the south and a Sunni Muslim minority (the ruling group under Saddam), the country was seen by some analysts as ripe for potential breakup. In his interview with Reuters, Syria's Bashar said he saw this outcome as unlikely but highly perilous. "The whole region has similar religious and ethnic divisions. It would be difficult to predict where it

U.S. Secretary of Defense Donald Rumsfeld ends the questioning at a Pentagon briefing while the U.S. commander of military operations in Afghanistan, Army General Tommy Franks, looks on, November 8, 2001. REUTERS

would end. If this did take place it would be the most dangerous thing that could happen."

Turkey's greatest fear was that a lunge for independence by Iraqi Kurds could revive secessionist aspirations among its own restive Kurds in the southeast, where more than 30,000 people had been killed since the Kurdistan Workers Party, also known by the initials PKK, began a campaign in 1984 for a Kurdish state. Saudi Arabia's rulers, linked to the strict Wahhabi sect, feared the emergence of any

Shi'ite power center in southern Iraq that could spur dissent among their own Shia minority.

Each country had something to gain. Kuwait could look forward to the removal of a threatening neighbor and possible resolution of unfinished Gulf War business, including the payment of reparations and the handover of Kuwaiti prisoners of war. The Kuwaitis and the Turks could anticipate U.S. rewards for the use of their military bases and airspace. The Saudis had a similar chance to repair U.S. ties—rocked by the September 11 attacks, in which 15 of the 19 hijackers were Saudi nationals—although Foreign Minister Prince Saud al-Faisal said the kingdom would only make such facilities available if the war had U.N. backing.

Jordan looked in line for substantial U.S. aid to compensate for the loss of cheap Iraqi oil and the jolt to its economy. Syria stood to benefit from piping Iraqi oil to the Mediterranean. And Iran could hope for a return of prisoners of war from its 1980–88 war with Iraq, an end to Iraqi support for its mujahideen opposition and a stronger political role for its Shia Muslim brethren inside Iraq.

Weighed against such hopes were two overriding fears. The first was that the United States could botch a war with Iraq and lose control of the unpredictable fallout, destabilizing the region and provoking waves of anger and unrest in countries that supported the U.S. action. The second was that Washington might succeed so completely that it might be encouraged to press ahead and pursue further "regime change" across the Middle East. Under that scenario, states such as Iran (like Iraq, a member of the "Axis of Evil") and Syria (with Iran and Libya, a permanent fixture on the list of states labeled by Washington as sponsors of terrorism) could find themselves next in line. "This is a nightmare for everyone except Israel and Turkey," said Mustafa Alani, Arab analyst at the Royal United Services Institute in London. A U.S. puppet government in Iraq could provide support and encouragement to the internal opposition in neighboring countries. And control of Iraqi oil would give Washington leverage over the entire regional economy and tip the power balance toward Israel, which could then dictate peace terms to its Arab enemies.

The Oil Factor

Some, beginning with the Iraqi government itself, see oil as the big prize for the United States and the secret driver of Washington's war agenda. According to this logic, Bush, a Texas oilman by background, is out to gain control of Iraq's reserves, the second largest in the world after Saudi Arabia. United States companies would be first in line to win lucrative exploration and production contracts, displacing French, Russian and Chinese firms that had signed agreements with Iraq under Saddam. According to U.S. government figures, Iraq produced 1.97 million barrels a day in the first seven months of 2002, down from a post-Gulf War peak of 2.57 million in 2000 and a high of 3.48 million in 1979. Iraqi oil sources said that output could rise by one million barrels a day within 18 months, given Western investment and the removal of sanctions. For Iraq to realize its full potential and hit its production target of six million bpd, estimates suggested close to $20 billion would need to be invested in its most promising oil fields in the south. The flow of all this extra oil onto world markets would sharply push down prices—to the advantage of the United States and the industrialized economies—and weaken or break the Saudi-led OPEC oil-producing cartel.

United Nations chief weapons inspector Hans Blix (right) speaks alongside U.S. Secretary of State Colin Powell and Mohamed ElBaradei, director-general of the International Atomic Energy Agency, after a meeting at the State Department in Washington, October 4, 2002. REUTERS

Some Arabs see this as a key part of the U.S. game plan. "If you control Iraqi reserves and Gulf states' reserves, you are in control of all supply, all production, all exports, so you can destroy OPEC, you can determine the price of oil," said Abdel Bari Atwan, London-based editor-in-chief of the Arabic newspaper *al-Quds*. "At the same time you can control the economy of Southeast Asia, Europe, the Third World, once you have your hands on the oil tap."

But most Western analysts doubt the theory that "it's really all about oil." If the United States wanted to push down the global price of oil with the help of increased Iraqi supply, a quicker way to do it would be to end sanctions against Baghdad instead of going to war. Instead, its military buildup had the short-term effect of creating nervousness and uncertainty on world markets and pushing prices higher. And some believed the short-term impact of war with Iraq could be to drive prices through the roof. Sheikh Zaki Yamani, the former Saudi oil minister, predicted oil would soar to $100 a barrel if Saddam responded to a U.S. attack by firing at Saudi Arabia and Kuwait, knocking out key oil facilities.

Oil conspiracy theories therefore looked overblown, but the long-term advantages to the United States of reducing energy dependence on Saudi Arabia and eroding OPEC pricing power were real. Oil, in the words of one U.S. analyst, was "not a disincentive" for Bush to attack Saddam. United States Commerce Department Under Secretary Grant Aldonas publicly acknowledged the potential benefits that would come from "opening up the spigot on Iraqi oil."

"That obviously isn't the point of any action taken against Saddam Hussein and Iraq, but certainly it would be one of the results economically," he said.

After Saddam, What Next?

Iraq's vast oil reserves were important for another reason: if Saddam were ousted and Western investment poured in, they would enable the country—unlike Afghanistan or the former Yugoslavia—to finance its recovery largely from its own resources. "It could be earning between $50 million and $60 million per day from oil," said Daniel Yergin, chairman of Cambridge Energy Research Associates. "It would mean an enormous resource for reconstruction, and especially if it wasn't diverting much of its revenues to financing a war machine."

But did the United States have a clear vision for a post-Saddam Iraq? If it did, it outlined it only in vague terms. The uncertainties

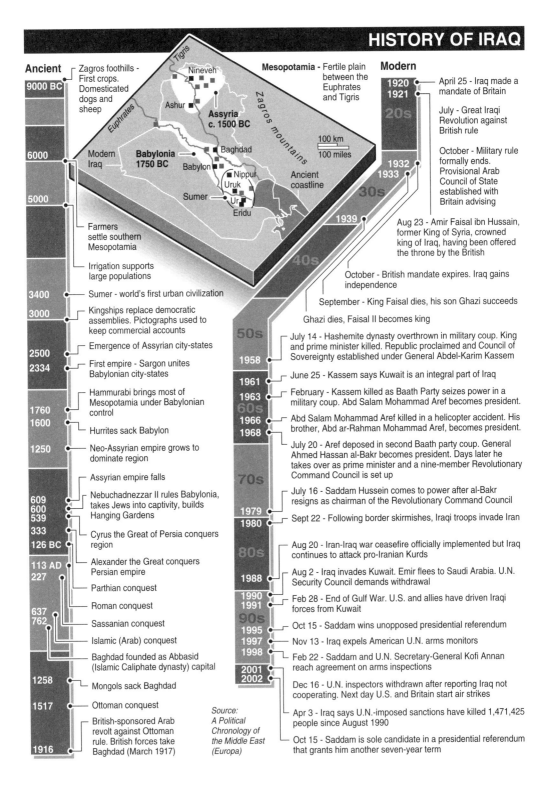

Ancient

9000 BC	Zagros foothills - First crops. Domesticated dogs and sheep
6000	Farmers settle southern Mesopotamia
5000	Irrigation supports large populations
3400	Sumer - world's first urban civilization
3000	Kingships replace democratic assemblies. Pictographs used to keep commercial accounts
2500	Emergence of Assyrian city-states
2334	First empire - Sargon unites Babylonian city-states
1760	Hammurabi brings most of Mesopotamia under Babylonian control
1600	Hurrites sack Babylon
1250	Neo-Assyrian empire grows to dominate region
	Assyrian empire falls
609	Nebuchadnezzar II rules Babylonia, takes Jews into captivity, builds Hanging Gardens
600	
539	
333	Cyrus the Great of Persia conquers region
126 BC	
113 AD	Alexander the Great conquers Persian empire
227	Parthian conquest
	Roman conquest
637	Sassanian conquest
762	Islamic (Arab) conquest
	Baghdad founded as Abbasid (Islamic Caliphate dynasty) capital
1258	Mongols sack Baghdad
1517	Ottoman conquest
1916	British-sponsored Arab revolt against Ottoman rule. British forces take Baghdad (March 1917)

Map labels:
Tigris
Nineveh
Ashur
Assyria c. 1500 BC
Zagros mountains
Modern Iraq
Euphrates
Babylonia 1750 BC
Baghdad
Babylon
Nippur
Uruk
Sumer
Ur
Eridu
Ancient coastline

Mesopotamia - Fertile plain between the Euphrates and Tigris

100 km
100 miles

Modern

1920	April 25 - Iraq made a mandate of Britain
1921	**20s** July - Great Iraqi Revolution against British rule
1932	October - Military rule formally ends. Provisional Arab Council of State established with Britain advising
1933	
	30s Aug 23 - Amir Faisal ibn Hussain, former King of Syria, crowned king of Iraq, having been offered the throne by the British
1939	October - British mandate expires. Iraq gains independence
	September - King Faisal dies, his son Ghazi succeeds
40s	Ghazi dies, Faisal II becomes king
50s	July 14 - Hashemite dynasty overthrown in military coup. King and prime minister killed. Republic proclaimed and Council of Sovereignty established under General Abdel-Karim Kassem
1958	
1961	June 25 - Kassem says Kuwait is an integral part of Iraq
1963	February - Kassem killed as Baath Party seizes power in a military coup. Abd Salam Mohammad Aref becomes president.
1966	**60s** Abd Salam Mohammad Aref killed in a helicopter accident. His brother, Abd ar-Rahman Mohammad Aref, becomes president.
1968	July 20 - Aref deposed in second Baath party coup. General Ahmed Hassan al-Bakr becomes president. Days later he takes over as prime minister and a nine-member Revolutionary Command Council is set up
	70s July 16 - Saddam Hussein comes to power after al-Bakr resigns as chairman of the Revolutionary Command Council
1979	
1980	Sept 22 - Following border skirmishes, Iraqi troops invade Iran
	80s Aug 20 - Iran-Iraq war ceasefire officially implemented but Iraq continues to attack pro-Iranian Kurds
1988	Aug 2 - Iraq invades Kuwait. Emir flees to Saudi Arabia. U.N. Security Council demands withdrawal
1990	Feb 28 - End of Gulf War. U.S. and allies have driven Iraqi forces from Kuwait
1991	
	90s Oct 15 - Saddam wins unopposed presidential referendum
1995	Nov 13 - Iraq expels American U.N. arms monitors
1997	
1998	Feb 22 - Saddam and U.N. Secretary-General Kofi Annan reach agreement on arms inspections
2001	Dec 16 - U.N. inspectors withdrawn after reporting Iraq not cooperating. Next day U.S. and Britain start air strikes
2002	Apr 3 - Iraq says U.N.-imposed sanctions have killed 1,471,425 people since August 1990
	Oct 15 - Saddam is sole candidate in a presidential referendum that grants him another seven-year term

*Source:
A Political
Chronology of
the Middle East
(Europa)*

involved were much the same as at the time of the Gulf War. Ironically it was Cheney himself, the former defense secretary and current vice president, who spelled these out in unmistakably clear terms when speaking to the BBC back in 1992: "If we'd gone to Baghdad and got rid of Saddam Hussein—assuming we could have found him—we'd have had to put a lot of forces in and run him to ground someplace. He would not have been easy to capture. Then you've got to put a new government in his place, and then you're faced with the question of what kind of government are you going to establish in Iraq? Is it going to be a Kurdish government or a Shia government or a Sunni government? How many forces are you going to have to leave there to keep it propped up, how many casualties are you going to take through the course of this operation?"

Those questions were as pointed and relevant in 2002 as they were a decade earlier, and the answers were far from obvious. One immediate model was Afghanistan: the United States had thrown its military backing behind the local opposition on the ground, quickly overthrown the ruling Taliban and overseen a political process leading to the installation of a pro-Western leader, Hamid Karzai. Could the same strategy work in Iraq, where numerous factions would compete to fill any post-Saddam vacuum?

As the largest opposition group on the ground, the Kurds control three of Iraq's eighteen provinces with some four million people. But they also present an obvious target of Saddam's revenge if the United States attacks Iraq, and many Kurds fear a repeat of his chemical weapons attacks on their region in 1988. The two main groups—the Kurdistan Democratic Party (KDP) of Massoud Barzani and the Patriotic Union of Kurdistan (PUK) of Jalal Talabani—have enjoyed de facto self-rule in northern Iraq since the Gulf War and now see a chance to win lasting autonomy within a new federal Iraq. But analysts see several risky scenarios. First, the KDP and PUK have a history of fighting each other, and any fresh bout of internal conflict could give Turkey a pretext to step in and crush the whole Kurdish movement. Second, the Kurdish factions may seek to expand their territorial control to oil-rich areas, especially Kirkuk, which could provide the economic foundation for a future Kurdish state. That, again, would be anathema to Turkey and would therefore be opposed by Ankara's ally, the United States.

The picture is messier still where the broader Iraqi opposition is concerned: the KDP and PUK are only two of six opposition groups recognized by Washington under the 1998 Iraq Liberation Act. Others

President George W. Bush and British Prime Minister Tony Blair answer questions from the media at Camp David, the presidential retreat in Maryland, September 7, 2002. REUTERS

are the Iraqi National Congress, led by former banker Ahmad Chalabi; the Iraqi National Accord of Ayad Allawi, a former member of Saddam's Baath Party; the Iran-based Supreme Council for Islamic Revolution in Iraq; and a monarchist movement headed by a distant relative of King Faisal, who was overthrown in 1958. Washington has renewed contacts with these disparate groups, which it had long dismissed as ineffective. There is no single obvious candidate to take charge of any new democratic government in Iraq.

The Future of America's War on Terrorism

One vision considered by the United States for a post-Saddam Iraq is, according to some reports, extended military occupation, as in Japan after World War Two. This raises questions about Washington's appetite for "nation building," its long-term commitment to stabilizing those countries where it intervenes, and its ability to fight a war on terror across a whole series of fronts around the globe.

By late 2002, the risks of overstretch were already becoming apparent, even before the start of any Iraq campaign. In Afghanistan, ostensibly Bush's greatest triumph to date, President Karzai came within inches of being assassinated in an episode that highlighted the country's continuing lawlessness and the risk of a fresh descent into civil war between rival factions and warlords. In Indonesia, a local Islamist group with links to al Qaeda was blamed for blowing up a Bali nightclub and killing some 180 people, mostly Australians. Critics asked if America, seemingly obsessed with Iraq, had taken its eye off the ball in Southeast Asia.

And then revelations emerged that North Korea had for years been pursuing a clandestine nuclear program and might already, according to Defense Secretary Rumsfeld, possess atomic weapons. Bush found his "Axis of Evil" logic being hurled back against him. Why was he bent on pursuing an Axis member that did not yet possess nuclear weapons in preference to one that quite possibly did?

More than one year into the war on terror, the enemy was unbroken and still active, though by no means solely against U.S. targets. A French supertanker was attacked with explosives off Yemen; a U.S. Marine was killed in Kuwait in an operation blamed on al Qaeda, and the CIA hit back by blowing up a car carrying a half-dozen suspected al Qaeda operatives in Yemen; Islamic militants from Chechnya held hundreds captive in a Moscow theater, and 128 of the hostages were killed when Russian special forces stormed the building after reportedly pumping in a "knockout gas" based on a powerful opiate.

Meanwhile the Israeli-Palestinian conflict rumbled on, alternating between spells of relative calm and wild spasms of violence as waves of Palestinian suicide bombings were met by crushing Israeli retaliation. Other conflicts, like that between the nuclear-armed duo of India and Pakistan, were quiescent but capable of re-erupting at any time.

Could the United States, the world's sole superpower, fight that many fires at once?

In the case of Iraq, many analysts believe that Bush has invested too much credibility and political capital to turn back now. The logic of his new security doctrine and the dictates of the war on terror, as he has defined it, make it likelier than not that he will press ahead against Saddam sooner or later.

At worst for the United States, some or all of the following could come to pass: conflict drags on with heavy U.S. and Iraqi civilian casualties; Saddam unleashes weapons of mass destruction on Israel, Kuwait and Saudi Arabia; the Arab street rises up in protest, undermining fragile, moderate governments such as Jordan's; Kurdish and Shi'ite revolts bring waves of refugees, the breakup of Iraq and a spillover of unrest around the region; oil supplies are disrupted and the price surge hits the world economy. Senior U.S. officials estimated the cost of war at somewhere between $100 billion and $200 billion, or up to 2 percent of U.S. Gross Domestic Product.

But the nightmare scenario is not the most likely, and few would bet against a quick U.S. military success. With a recent track record of crushing victories in the Gulf War, Kosovo and Afghanistan, the world's most powerful and technologically advanced army should sweep aside Saddam's forces. If and when that happens, some of Bush's critics may fall silent. Even those countries most hostile to the United States will tread carefully for fear of becoming next in line for "regime change."

But victory in the wider war on terror is a different matter entirely. Among the chief reasons stated by bin Laden for waging holy war against the United States are U.S. persecution of Iraq, the suffering of Palestinians at the hands of Israel (armed and funded by the United States), and the U.S. military presence in Saudi Arabia, seen as defiling the land of the Prophet. These are the festering, unresolved grievances that drive new recruits to al Qaeda. They may only be aggravated, not diminished, by U.S.-led war on Iraq.

Saddam's Iron Grip on Power

Patrick Worsnip

From the air, as our helicopter approached, it looked at first like many another Middle Eastern towns: flat-roofed, breezeblock houses clustered around a few streets. It was only as we closed in that we saw what was unusual about it. It was broad daylight, but there were no people moving about, no vehicles except for a few military trucks. The only real sign of life was the occasional cow or sheep staggering drunkenly down the streets between what we saw now were badly damaged buildings. Something terrible had happened here.

This was Halabja, the town in Iraqi Kurdistan that was to go down in history as the place where a government had used chemical weapons against its own people. It was March 1988, and the Iran-Iraq war was into its eighth year. The war seemed to be going the way of Iraq but the Iranians were still dangerous and, with the help of local Kurdish militias opposed to the Baghdad government, had captured a corner of northeastern Iraq of which Halabja was the main prize. In revenge, the Iraqi air force struck back on March 16, devastating the town and its people with conventional explosives and poison gas. But Halabja remained in Iranian hands, and the Tehran government, anxious for a propaganda coup, had invited in the foreign press to witness what the Iraqis had done. I was among the first Western journalists to get there.

Our Iranian army Chinook helicopter landed in a field just outside the town. We had flown from Kermanshah in western Iran, hugging the contours of the Zagros Mountains, green and deceptively peaceful in the mild spring weather, to avoid detection by Iraqi warplanes. We scrambled out, and our Iranian escorts took us straight into the center of Halabja, or what was left of it. Awkward in our Western civilian clothes, we picked our way through the debris and tried to piece together from our guides and from a few survivors who emerged from the ruins exactly what had happened.

One thing, in any case, was very clear—a lot of people had been killed. Bodies were strewn everywhere, stiff from rigor mortis and looking, as I wrote in my dispatch to Reuters, "like wax dolls." In one house, an entire family lay where they had perished around a meal table. And yet the bodies, and the brightly colored Kurdish clothes

RELIGIOUS AND ETHNIC DIVISIONS IN IRAQ

Islam – meaning "submission" to God's will – was founded by the Prophet Mohammad between 610 and 632 A.D.
The scripture of Islam is the Koran, believed to be literally the word of God

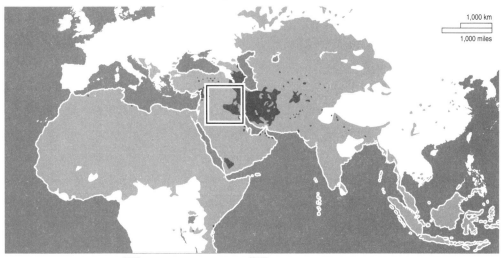

1,000 km

1,000 miles

After the Prophet's death, the Islamic world split into two main factions, later known as Sunni and Shi'ite, which disputed the succession to Mohammad

Sunni Muslims
Follow the "sunna," or the teachings of the Prophet, and the legitimacy of the orthodox Caliphs (successors) chosen to lead Muslims after his death

Shi'ite Muslims
Shi'ites believe that Ali, the cousin and son-in-law of Mohammad, who eventually became the fourth Caliph, should have been the Prophet's immediate successor. They consider Ali the first in a line of 12 Imams, the last of whom did not die but disappeared and will one day reappear to rule the world

Sunni   Shi'ite   Kurds – Non-Arab, mainly Sunni Muslim

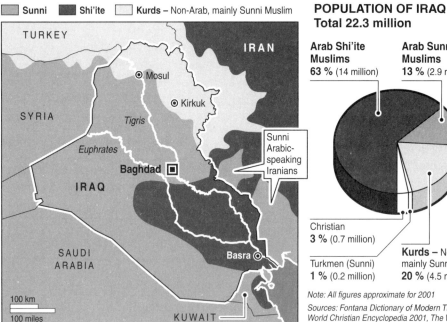

TURKEY

IRAN

⊙ Mosul

⊙ Kirkuk

SYRIA

Tigris

Euphrates

Baghdad ▣

IRAQ

Sunni Arabic-speaking Iranians

SAUDI ARABIA

Basra ⊙

KUWAIT

100 km

100 miles

POPULATION OF IRAQ
Total 22.3 million

Arab Shi'ite Muslims
63 % (14 million)

Arab Sunni Muslims
13 % (2.9 million)

Christian
3 % (0.7 million)

Turkmen (Sunni)
1 % (0.2 million)

Kurds – Non-Arab, mainly Sunni Muslim
20 % (4.5 million)

Note: All figures approximate for 2001

Sources: Fontana Dictionary of Modern Thought, World Christian Encyclopedia 2001, The World Almanac 2002, The Statesman's Yearbook 2003

they were dressed in, were virtually unmarked. They had died, we were told, of a lethal cocktail of chemical weapons—mustard gas, cyanide and nerve gas. Outside in the street was the body of a man clutching the corpse of an infant—a photograph of them has become one of the best-known testimonies of the Halabja massacre.

The Iranians told us that 5,000 people had been killed altogether, a figure now accepted as fact. Arriving nearly a week after the event, we had no way of checking it, and ourselves saw perhaps only a few hundred bodies. The Iraqis denied responsibility. But in Halabja, no one was in any doubt who was to blame. It was daubed on the walls—those that were still standing—in Farsi and Arabic: *Marg bar Saddam*, *Al-Mout li Saddam*—"Death to Saddam."

Saddam Outlasts His Foes

Saddam Hussein al-Tikriti, President of the Republic of Iraq, has dominated the country's politics for the last quarter of a century. The name Saddam is unusual in the Arab world. And yet, entirely due to one man, it is perhaps the most familiar Arab name in the West today. In any inhabited part of Iraq it is impossible to escape his presence. The craggy, mustachioed face looks out like George Orwell's Big Brother from building walls and advertisement hoardings, and from statues in town squares. Saddam Hussein has become the face of Iraq.

During his years in power, Saddam has led Iraq into two wars—the war against Iran from 1980–88 and the Gulf War of early 1991 sparked off by his invasion of Kuwait in August 1990. He has brought poverty, suffering and death to a country that, sitting on the world's second largest proven oil reserves, enjoying ample water resources and possessed of an educated elite, could have been one of the most prosperous and powerful in the region. In any democracy, and in many autocracies, such mistakes would have brought certain downfall. But while Saddam has lost control of Kurdistan, and his activities in both the north and the south of Iraq have been curtailed by the Western imposition of "no-fly zones" since soon after the Gulf War, his grip on power in Baghdad at the head of one of the world's most ruthless police states is as strong as ever. He has outlasted foes ranging from Ayatollah Ruhollah Khomeini in Iran to President George Bush senior of the United States. In an October 2002 referendum, 100 percent of the electorate voted for Saddam to continue as president for another seven years, the regime claimed. He was the sole candidate. This is the country that is preparing to confront the world's mightiest power, the United States, in a possible second Gulf War stemming from Iraq's alleged chemical, biological and nuclear weapons programs.

Cradle of Civilization

The country called Iraq has existed in its present borders for less than a century. But although associated in the Western mind nowadays with oil, weapons of mass destruction and Saddam Hussein, the territory it covers is a cradle of civilization. It was long known as Mesopotamia, Greek for the "land between the rivers"—the Tigris and the Euphrates that are still its predominant natural features.

It was here that, perhaps as early as 3500 BC, the Sumerians created one of the world's first urban civilizations and developed cuneiform writing. Later, the Assyrian empire arose in what is now Kurdistan, with its fabled city of Nineveh close to present-day Mosul. Babylon, whose King Nebuchadnezzar ruled in Biblical times, was

Iraqi schoolgirls dance in front of a painting of Saddam at the top of an Iraqi map during a school gathering in Baghdad, October 1, 2002. Iraq was preparing to vote in a referendum for another seven-year term for Saddam. REUTERS

located about 55 miles south of Baghdad. Its Hanging Gardens were one of the seven wonders of the ancient world.

After more than a millennium in which Mesopotamia was a battleground between the great powers of antiquity, the Arab Muslims arrived in the 7th century. The Abbasid caliphs set up their capital in Baghdad, which reached the zenith of its prosperity under Haroun al-Rashid in the late 8th century, when it was considered the richest

Iraqi women walk past a mosaic of Saddam in Baghdad's Al-Askan district, January 4, 1999. Pictures of the Iraqi president are posted on every public building and on the main streets, dominating the city of Baghdad. REUTERS

city in the world. Many of the stories from *The Arabian Nights* are set there. The curtain only came down when the Mongols destroyed both Baghdad and the caliphate in 1258. The Ottoman Turks took control of Iraq in the 16th century and held it until World War One, when the country's modern history begins.

After Turkey allied itself with Germany and declared war on Britain and France, Britain invaded Iraq, primarily to defend the oil interests it had recently acquired in the region, notably in Iran. It was perhaps the first, but was to be by no means the last, time that oil considerations had been a prelude to military action in Iraq. By early 1918 British forces had captured the Ottoman provinces of Basra, Baghdad and Mosul, which were to form present-day Iraq. The Ottoman Empire collapsed and, under a post-war Middle East carveup with France, Britain was awarded a mandate over Iraq, along with Jordan and Palestine (France took Syria and Lebanon). In 1921, Britain established a monarchy in Iraq under King Faisal, and in 1932 it granted the country independence, although it was no secret to anyone that London continued to pull the strings from behind the scenes. Faisal died the following year and was succeeded by his son Ghazi.

Tikrit: Impoverished and Violent

Such was the country into which Saddam Hussein was born—on April 28, 1937, according to the Iraqi government, perhaps two years later in the view of some historians, who believe that the Iraqi leader may have wished to conceal that he had married a woman older than himself.

There is no dispute about the place of Saddam's birth—the village of Al-Awja near the impoverished and violent town of Tikrit, in the northern part of the Sunni Muslim belt of central Iraq. Then, as now, the mix of races and religions in the country that the British had created was one of the main complicating factors in its politics. More than half of Iraqis, concentrated in the south of the country, adhere to the Shi'ite branch of Islam, which is also the dominant religion in neighboring Iran. About one-fifth, living in the north, are Kurds, who speak a language related to Persian and whose most famous son, Saladin, the Muslim commander who trounced the Christian Crusaders in the 12th century, also came from Tikrit. The rest are Sunni Muslims, and it was them, or rather their privileged upper class, that the British chose to be the rulers of Iraq.

Saddam's clan, however, were poor, lower-class Sunnis with no pretensions to political power and a grudge against the established order. There were also family problems that some biographers have seen as typical of future dictators. Saddam's father, Hussein al-Majid, disappeared and may have died before he was born, and he was brought up in a one-room house by his mother, Subha, and her second husband. Saddam's relations with his stepfather were poor, and at the age of eight or ten he went to live with his maternal uncle, Khairallah, in a nearby village. It was a move that not only changed his life, but may also have changed the course of Middle East history. Khairallah, a former army officer, who had been cashiered after the British put down a pro-Nazi rebellion in Iraq during World War Two and who had then become a teacher, sent Saddam to school, where he proved a fast learner. Saddam later married Khairallah's daughter, his first cousin Sajida.

In the early 1950s, Khairallah moved to Baghdad, taking his nephew with him. Saddam's teenage years were influenced by popular

An Iraqi Kurd boy rests by a bullet-pocked wall displaying a painting of Saddam in the northern Iraqi town of Zakho near the Turkish border, April 1991. REUTERS

hostility to the monarchy and the pro-British elite that supported it and by admiration for Gamal Abdel Nasser, the Arab nationalist who had taken over in Egypt. As a student leader of antigovernment protests he set up gangs of toughs who beat up those who refused to join their protests. It was a sign of things to come. By the late 1950s, Saddam had gravitated to the Iraqi branch of the Baath Party, which had been founded during World War Two by a Syrian Christian named Michel Aflaq and which preached the creation of a single socialist Arab nation. In 1958, a group of "free officers" in the Iraqi army overthrew the monarchy and proclaimed a republic.

The Baathists soon fell out with the new authorities, and Saddam was selected to take part in an attempt to assassinate Prime Minister Abdel Karim Kassem. The ambush failed and Saddam fled, wounded, to Syria. He moved to Cairo, where he attended law school, returning to Iraq after the Baathists finally toppled Kassem and seized power in 1963. Saddam reportedly took part in bloody reprisals against Kassem supporters, but before the year was out the Baathists had been ousted.

In 1964, Saddam was arrested and spent nearly two years in jail before escaping by bribing the driver of a prison van. In a split soon afterward with the Syrian Baathists, Saddam and his long-time mentor

Britain released this picture of what it said was the aftermath of an Iraqi chemical attack on the town of Halabja in 1988 as part of a dossier to set up a case for military action against Iraq, September 24, 2002. REUTERS

Ahmed Hassan al-Bakr, a relative from Tikrit, set up their own national command of the party for Iraq. In 1968, Saddam, riding a tank, took part in a fresh Baathist coup that deposed the government of President Abd ar-Rahman Mohammad Aref. Bakr became the new president, and within six months Saddam was vice president, taking charge of, among other things, the security services.

Before long it was clear that Saddam was the real power in Iraq. Bakr delegated much of the day-to-day running of the country to him after suffering a heart attack in 1976 and in July 1979 stepped down, probably under pressure, to make way for his protégé.

Counting on Quick Victory

It was just over a year later, September 22, 1980. I was sitting in the Reuters office in Tehran, considering the plight of 52 American diplomats who had been held hostage for more than 10 months by Iranian Islamic militants. The phone rang, and my Iranian colleague, Ali, answered it. He put down the phone and turned to me.

"That was my brother, who works at Tehran airport," he said. "Iraqi planes have just bombed it."

Soon afterward, word came through that Iraqi armor had thrust across the southwest Iranian border into the oil-producing province of Khuzestan. There had been border skirmishing for months, but few had expected an all-out war. Nor did we expect that the war that had now erupted would go on for eight years, one of the longest wars of the 20th century. No one knows precisely how many died, but Western estimates reckon more than 100,000 Iraqis and a quarter of a million Iranians were slain in the conflict. Saddam Hussein, the man who had

A young Iraqi Kurdish girl holds her hand and a bowl out for food as she sits with other family members in a sprawling mountain refugee camp in Isikveren, Turkey, April 7, 1991. REUTERS

launched it, did not expect that, either. He was counting on a quick victory over the feuding mullahs in Tehran and an end to what he saw as Iranian subversion among the Shi'ite majority in southern Iraq. But then Saddam had reckoned without the stubbornness of Khomeini, the man he had expelled not so long ago from his Iraqi exile.

Modest Education, Deprived Background

How did a man of modest education from a deprived background come to reach supreme power in Iraq at the age of little more than 40 and then hold onto it far longer than any predecessor, becoming one of the Arab world's great survivors? Innate shrewdness and a fair slice of luck undoubtedly played a major role, but one thing that distinguishes Saddam from most other leaders on the world stage has been not just his ruthless use of force to achieve his goals but his willingness to take part himself. There is a long history of settling disputes in Iraq—ranging from family quarrels to political rivalries—at the point of a gun, and even today many Iraqis see Saddam as, at heart, a street fighter who will bring a street fighter's instincts to any showdown with the United States.

Saddam has shown his taste for violence from his early days as a gang leader to his reported personal role in killing off rivals after his assumption of the presidency. In the most widely reported incident, Saddam shot dead his health minister, Riyadh Ibrahim, during a cabinet meeting in March 1982, although accounts vary over the reason. Some versions say Ibrahim had suggested Saddam might step aside temporarily so that peace negotiations could be started with Iran. Others, partly backed up in an official announcement of Ibrahim's execution, say he had been raking off a percentage from the import of defective medicines.

Whatever the truth, repression of dissenters and rebellious groups remains key to the regime's grip on power. Reports by the human rights organization Amnesty International speak year after year of arbitrary arrest, systematic torture and execution without formal trial.

Under recent decrees, Amnesty says, women have been beheaded for alleged prostitution, and men have had their tongues cut out for slandering the president.

Similar methods writ large have been employed to crush ethnic and religious groups thought to pose a threat to Saddam's rule. Halabja was only the tip of the iceberg of Baghdad's use of chemical weapons against the Kurds, attracting attention because it was the only place Western journalists were able to visit while the evidence was still fresh. Poison gas was used throughout Kurdistan during the course of 1988 in an operation dubbed al-Anfal, after a section of the Koran celebrating the Prophet Mohammad's first military victory in 624. Saddam's cousin Ali Hassan al-Majeed, whom he had appointed governor of the North, directed the Kurdish operation. According to Western and Kurdish estimates, about 150,000–200,000 people were killed, nearly 4,000 villages destroyed and tens of thousands of people deported south.

Saddam put his cousin back to work to suppress a potentially much more dangerous uprising by southern Shi'ites just days after Iraq had surrendered to the U.S.-led coalition in the Gulf War in 1991. At least 50,000 people, and possibly many more, are thought to have died, although the rebels treated the Baathists they captured with equal brutality before Majid reoccupied their key cities. In a further move against the Shi'ites three months later, Saddam's troops killed thousands and forcibly relocated up to 150,000 "Marsh Arabs" who had rebelled against his plan to drain the wetlands they lived in at the confluence of the Tigris and Euphrates.

Iraqi Kurdish men and boys grab bread as they swarm over a truck distributing food in the Isikveren refugee camp in Turkey, April 7, 1991. REUTERS

The Ties that Bind

If unrest in the regions has posed a repeated threat to Saddam's hold on power, he has proved adept at fending off the palace revolutions that previously plagued Iraq. The Baathists' own putsch in 1968 was the country's last successful coup, although there have been plenty of failed attempts since then, according to reports filtering out of the country. In this sense, Saddam and his associates have brought stability of a kind, and part of the explanation can be found in the nature of the Baath Party. Although in Iraq it depends partly on family

Iraqi Kurdish refugees gather pieces of bread from a dirt road to feed family members in the Isikveren refugee camp in Turkey, April 7, 1991. REUTERS

connections, its highly organized structure, methods and revolutionary rhetoric are reminiscent of, and to a certain extent modeled on, the communist parties of the former Soviet Union and Eastern Europe. Like them, it could brook no opposition, and one of the rival parties it repressed was, ironically, the pro-Moscow Iraqi Communist Party. Significantly, Baathist rule under an autocratic leader brought stability at about the same time to Iraq's equally coup-prone neighbor, Syria.

The early years of Baathism also brought Iraq an economic expansion perhaps unparalleled since the Middle Ages. Saddam himself directed the nationalization of the all-important oil industry in 1972, and the oil price boom resulting from the Arab–Israeli war of the following year brought a massive influx of petrodollars into the nation's coffers. Gross domestic product more than quadrupled between 1968 and 1979, allowing the state to maintain a generous welfare system. Imports of both consumer and industrial goods spiraled, making Iraq by the end of the 1970s one of the most important Middle Eastern markets for the West and Japan along with Iran and Saudi Arabia. The state, as principal investor, saw its role in the economy grow hugely, but private capital also benefited, creating a new class with a stake in the system. Saddam built a modern infrastructure, an efficient health system and good schools. A new middle class emerged whose members were allowed to prosper as long as they stayed out of politics.

The two wars that Iraq has fought, and the U.N. sanctions imposed in 1990 and continuing in 2002, have done away with all that. Per capita income, more than $4,000 in 1980, had fallen below $500 by 1993 because of the Gulf War. Inflation of up to 1,000 percent a year has rendered the currency virtually worthless. Diseases such as cholera, typhoid and diphtheria have reappeared or greatly increased. Government propaganda has highlighted malnutrition among children and blamed the sanctions and their Western sponsors. Some three million Iraqis—about 15 percent of the population—have emigrated, many of them middle-class professionals. A so-called "oil-for-food" program was introduced by the United Nations in 1996, under which Iraq can export oil and import food and medicine. Iraq says the program has had little effect on the plight of the nation.

Chronology of Modern Iraq

1920

Apr 25   Iraq is made a mandate of the United Kingdom.

Jul   A revolt against British rule takes place, known as the Great Iraqi Revolution.

Oct   A provisional Arab Council of State is established with Britain advising after military rule is formally ended.

1921

Aug 23   Amir Faisal ibn Hussain, former King of Syria, is crowned king, having been offered the throne by the British.

1932

Oct   Britain's mandate runs out and Iraq becomes independent.

1933

Sep   King Faisal dies and is succeeded by his son Ghazi.

1939

Apr   Ghazi dies in a car crash and Faisal II becomes king.

1958

Jul 14   The Hashemite dynasty is overthrown in a military coup and both King Faisal and his prime minister, Nuri al Said, are killed. A republic is proclaimed and a Council of Sovereignty established under General Abdel-Karim Kassem.

1961

Jun 25   General Kassem says that Kuwait is an integral part of Iraq.

1963

Feb   The Baath Party seizes power in a military coup, and General Kassem is killed. His former coup partner, Abd Salam Mohammad Aref, becomes president.

1968

Jul 20   President Abd ar-Rahman Mohammad Aref, who had succeeded his brother, Abd Salam Mohammad Aref, who was killed in a helicopter accident in 1966, is deposed in a coup mounted by the Baath Party, and General Ahmed Hassan al-Bakr becomes president. Days later he takes over as prime minister, and a nine-member Revolutionary Command Council is set up.

1979

Jul 16   Saddam Hussein comes to power after President Ahmed Hassan al-Bakr resigns as chairman of the Revolutionary Command Council.

1980

Sep 22   Iraqi troops invade Iran.

1981

Jun 7   Israeli warplanes destroy Iraq's Osirak nuclear reactor.

1988

Aug 20   A ceasefire is officially implemented in the Iran–Iraq war, but Iraq continues to attack pro-Iranian Kurds.

1990

Aug 2   Iraq invades Kuwait at 2 a.m. (2300 GMT Aug 1). Emir flees to Saudi Arabia. The U.N. Security Council condemns Iraqi occupation 14–0 and demands Baghdad withdraw.

(continued)

1991

Jan 17   U.S.-led allied forces start Gulf War by launching an air and missile offensive against Iraqi positions and installations in Iraq and occupied Kuwait.

Feb 28   Hostilities end with the United States and allies having driven Iraqi forces from Kuwait. Later in the year U.S., British and French planes start patrolling Iraq's northern skies to shield Iraq's Kurds from attack by Baghdad.

1992

Dec   Saddam expresses desire for new relationship with Washington following U.S. President Bush's election defeat.

1995

Oct 15   Saddam wins a presidential referendum and is elected unopposed with more than 99 percent of the vote.

1997

Nov 13   Iraq expels American arms monitors.

1998

Feb 22   U.N. Secretary-General Kofi Annan reaches agreement with Iraq on arms inspections after meeting Saddam in Baghdad.

Dec 16   U.N. inspectors withdrawn from Baghdad a day after reporting Iraq was still not cooperating with their work.

Dec 17   U.S. and Britain start air strikes against Iraq.

2000

Aug 23   Iraq says it will not accept the new United Nations arms inspection team established under a Security Council resolution of December 1999.

2001

Jan 25   The U.N. Gulf War reparations body says it has paid out $1.46 billion to those who proved losses inflicted by Iraq, bringing the total to this date to $11 billion.

2002

Jun 16   President Bush allows the CIA conduct covert operations to topple Saddam.

Oct   Mohammed Aldouri, Iraq's ambassador to the United Nations, says that 1.7 million people have died as a result of U.N. sanctions.

Oct 12   An adviser to Saddam sends a letter to U.N. weapons inspectors saying Iraq is ready to remove all obstacles to a return of inspectors after nearly four years. The next day the United States dismisses the latest Iraqi offer.

Oct 15   Saddam is the only candidate in a referendum that grants him another seven-year term.

Oct 20   Iraq begins releasing political prisoners under an unprecedented amnesty issued by Saddam to inmates and exiles to mark his 100 percent win in an uncontested referendum on October 15.

Nov 8   U.N. Security Council unanimously approves a resolution giving Iraq one last chance to eliminate its weapons of mass destruction or face "serious consequences."

Nov 13   Iraq accepts U.N. resolution 1441 and says it is awaiting U.N. weapons inspectors resolution.

Nov 18   Advance party of U.N. inspectors land in Baghdad for first time in four years.

Iraqi troops parade before Saddam in Baghdad, December 31, 2000. REUTERS

Seeds of Crisis

The events that brought Iraq to this pass and sowed the seeds of the present crisis began with the Iraqi invasion of Kuwait on August 2, 1990. Saddam did not think up Iraq's territorial claim to Kuwait, which borders it to the south. President Kassem had advanced it in the past, and before him King Ghazi. But neither of them had resorted to military action. Saddam's reasoning has been much discussed, but he apparently thought that he could right a perceived historical wrong, put his million-man army left over from the Iran–Iraq war to work and add Kuwait's oil wealth to Iraq's own to boost economic recovery—and that the outside world would acquiesce. The assumption proved utterly wrong and put Saddam on a collision course with a U.S. administration that had previously been prepared to overlook—even connive at—his actions in the region. As Reuters Diplomatic Correspondent at the time, I was at the meeting that marked the end of attempts to find a peaceful way out.

The diplomatic drama unfolded on January 9, 1991, at the Intercontinental Hotel in Geneva. U.S. Secretary of State James Baker was seeking from Iraqi Foreign Minister Tareq Aziz a climb-down that would head off a threatened U.S.-led onslaught to drive Iraqi forces out of Kuwait. I was among a horde of journalists pacing the corridors hoping for some clue as to how the talks were going. There was none, although rumors abounded. The day-long negotiations ended, and the two principals called a news conference. Aziz spoke first, but his remarks were inconclusive. Then Baker took the microphone. For about a minute, he described how he and Aziz had sought to strike a deal.

"Regrettably..." he went on—but no one listened any further. That one word—"regrettably"—had said it all. The talks had failed.

Iraqi Deputy Prime Minister Tareq Aziz gestures under a picture of Saddam as he addresses reporters during a news conference at the Ministry of Information in Baghdad, September 14, 2002. REUTERS

Traders around the world, watching live on CNN, hit their screen keyboards, in a frenzy of buying and selling in anticipation of war. It was to be another week before U.S. bombers went into action, but the countdown to war in the Gulf had already begun.

The Great Survivor

Saddam's survival of defeat in the Gulf War, followed immediately by Kurdish and Shi'ite insurrections, represented his supreme act of political escapology and testified to the tight hold he has established on the country. It is based on a combination of fear and privilege: U.N. sanctions had little impact on Saddam's entourage, family and clan. Saddam's kith and kin from Tikrit helped him to power and were rewarded.

Tikritis had long been numerous in the Iraqi army, a factor that was to prove important as the military was increasingly drawn into politics after World War Two. One of them was Ahmed Hassan al-Bakr, who became Saddam's stepping stone to supreme power. Another was Saddam's uncle Khairallah, who ultimately became mayor of Baghdad and whose son, Adnan, was made army chief of staff and defense minister. His cousin Ali Hassan al-Majeed also served as defense minister and led operations to crush insurgents. One of Saddam's half-brothers has served as interior minister and another as secret police chief. Other relatives have received lesser roles.

Saddam has been careful to recruit loyalists from elsewhere, however, to broaden the base of his regime. Tareq Aziz, for example, the deputy prime minister, is a Christian who speaks fluent English and for years has been the international face of the Iraqi government. Iraq experts say Saddam has also played skillfully on divisions within the Kurdish and Shi'ite communities to keep them under control.

"He has shown extraordinary skill at knowing whom to trust and when," says Charles Tripp of London's School of Oriental and African Studies. "He mistrusts everybody, but it's more complex than that. He knows what makes the people around him tick."

Family favoritism has had its limits, with Saddam showing no mercy to relatives who betrayed him. In 1995, his two sons-in-law,

Hussein and Saddam Kamel, defected to Jordan with their wives—Saddam's daughters Raghid and Rana—and children. Hussein, in particular, a former minister in charge of military industries, was a key catch for the West and was extensively debriefed by the U.S. Central Intelligence Agency. But he was not taken up by the United States as a potential future president of Iraq, as he had apparently hoped, and found little welcome in Amman. Almost unbelievably, the sons-in-law returned to Iraq in February 1996 with their families, possibly lured by promises of an amnesty. The outcome was inevitable. A few days later, Hussein and Saddam Kamel were shot dead along with several relatives by what the official media said were angry clansmen out to avenge tribal honor.

Saddam is flanked by his two sons, Uday (left) and Qusay, in this file photo released by the Iraqi government, December 13, 1996. Uday had been seriously wounded the previous day when gunmen opened fire on his car in Baghdad. Official handout.

In recent years, attention has focused on Saddam's two sons, Uday and Qusay, partly because—barring U.S. intervention—the eventual presidential succession in Iraq is likely to be kept within the family, as has already happened in Syria with the ruling Assad dynasty. What is known of the two brothers suggests little prospect of change if either were to take over. Saddam Kamel, during his defection to Jordan, described the elder son, Uday (born 1964), as "reckless, murderous and licentious." Kamel also said Uday had killed one of Saddam's bodyguards in a petty quarrel and shot and wounded his own uncle, Watban, over a business dispute. Uday nearly died in an assassination attempt in 1996, suffering eight bullet wounds from which he has never fully recovered. He has been allowed to run Iraq's lucrative

Saddam's elder son, Uday, holds a hunting rifle on a boat in Iraq in this undated picture released December 14, 2000, by the Iraqi Olympic Committee (chaired by Uday) to mark the fourth anniversary of a failed assassination attempt on Uday on December 12, 1996. Official handout.

import-export ministries and also controls a newspaper, *Babel* (Babylon). The quieter Qusay (born 1966) may be a more credible successor. He runs the Special Security Organization, the top security unit in Iraq, and commands the 15,000-strong Special Republican Guard, the troops most loyal to Saddam.

Personality Cult

Many of the traits of Saddam and the regime he runs are familiar from similar figures throughout history. The official images of Saddam—riding a white charger, brandishing a golden sword, firing a Kalashnikov assault rifle—often strike Westerners as grotesque expressions of the personality cult that surrounds him. But Saddam is not interested in what the West thinks, say those who have studied him. The Palestinian author Said K. Aburish, who has written an authoritative biography of Saddam, *Saddam Hussein: The Politics of Revenge*, sees a parallel with the Soviet dictator Stalin. "He (Saddam) has modeled himself after and adopted the ways of Joseph Stalin and merged them with his tribal instincts," Aburish writes. "This synthesis of Bedouin guile and Communist method, a unique combination, is what confuses both his friends and his adversaries."

Arguably, Saddam's cat-and-mouse games with U.N. arms inspectors during the 1990s, which ended in their departure from Iraq in 1998, are an illustration of that point. In his fixation with clinging to power, while plunging his country into ruinous wars, some commentators have also compared Saddam to the former Yugoslav leader Slobodan Milosevic—indeed, the two countries are reported to have consulted on ways of resisting U.S. bombing. But few expect Saddam to end up, like Milosevic, before a war crimes tribunal in The Hague.

A day before the referendum that extended Saddam's rule, an Iraqi boy looks at a painting of his country's leader in Baghdad, October 14, 2002. REUTERS

The British Labour Party parliamentarian George Galloway, a frequent visitor to Baghdad who has met the Iraqi leader twice, says Saddam the man contrasts with Saddam the icon portrayed by the regime: "He's quite a shy person, not at all bombastic, whilst the personality cult built around him is deliberately constructed to make him look incredibly bombastic and egomaniacal," Galloway told me. "He's got a soft handshake when you expect a brutal one. He speaks quietly, he doesn't speak a lot, he listens. I would describe him as a messianic kind of man in the sense that his discourse seldom deals with the facts, the ABCs and the todays and tomorrows. He likes to talk about things that happened many hundreds of years ago and things that will happen many hundreds of years from now."

According to Galloway, who opposes U.S. and British policy on Iraq, Saddam has survived this long because he has solid support among the Sunni Muslim and Christian communities, and enough support among the Shi'ites to keep them quiet. "I think the West fantastically underestimates the level of popularity that Saddam Hussein has," he said. "Millions of people in Iraq no doubt hate their president, but millions don't." Washington and London, however, say that the first to benefit from Saddam's overthrow would be the Iraqi people.

Few if any of Saddam's fellow Arab leaders have much enthusiasm for him or would be sorry to see him go—if this could happen in a way that would not disturb the balance of power in the region. But for many Arabs in the street, the West's policy toward Iraq is marked by hypocrisy.

As they looked at the Gulf in 1980, Western powers could see only one serious threat: Iran, whose Islamic revolution threatened instability from Morocco in the west to Indonesia in the east. They were only too happy to look the other way while Iraq attacked Iran and to quietly support Baghdad's war effort. A British military attaché in Jordan boasted to me in 1982 of how British engineers were refurbishing Chieftain tanks captured by the Iraqis from Iran, so that they could be turned back against the Iranians. Of course, an all-out Iraqi victory might be destabilizing too, so the stalemate that developed was no catastrophe. It kept the two most formidable military powers in the region occupied, and the oil continued to flow. Even the atrocity at Halabja failed to stir much indignation in Western capitals at the time. So as Arabs see it, when the Iran–Iraq war ended and Saddam sent his army into Kuwait, changing overnight from a friendly dictator into an ogre, the West had to take its share of the blame.

Saddam fires a rifle during a pro-Palestinian military parade in Baghdad, November 20, 2000. REUTERS

Combination picture shows some of the multitude of portraits of Iraqi President Saddam Hussein decorating the walls of Baghdad, February 4, 2001. REUTERS

Arabs argue, the United States is obsessed about Iraq's weapons of mass destruction but does nothing about Israel's. It insists that Iraq comply with U.N. resolutions but allows the Jewish state to ignore other resolutions calling for Israeli withdrawal from Arab land. So, Saddam is a tyrant? Well, other Arab leaders in favor in the West also use strong-arm methods against their domestic opponents.

When Saddam fired Scud missiles at Tel Aviv during the Gulf War, some Palestinians cheered. Yasser Arafat's Palestine Liberation Organization did itself serious diplomatic damage by failing to condemn Iraq's seizure of Kuwait. The inherent weakness of many Arab states is the gulf between populations radicalized by poverty and official corruption on the one hand, and, on the other, undemocratic governments trying to stay in favor with the West while keeping the lid on dissent at home.

Iraqis have many things for which they can blame Saddam Hussein. But that he is a puppet of the United States, they cannot say—although he may have enjoyed covert U.S. support at certain periods in the past. As many an autocrat before Saddam has understood, spitting defiance at the enemy will always ensure some backing at home. The question is whether, if it comes to a U.S. invasion, the Iraqi people will, as the government says it will, defend the country street by street and house by house or simply cut its losses and leave Saddam to his fate.

The Gulf War:
Dispatches from the Front Line

Paul Holmes

"We were 150 miles away from Baghdad and there was nobody between us and Baghdad. If it had been our intention to overrun the country, we could have done it unopposed."

General Norman Schwarzkopf

"Applaud your victory, my dear citizens. You have faced 30 countries and the evil they have brought here. In this mother of all battles we have succeeded in harvesting what we have sown."

Iraqi President Saddam Hussein

Suddenly and uncharacteristically my driver, an Iraqi Christian who went by the name of George, decided he had something to get off his chest.

"Look at the bridge," he said as we passed one of the spans across the Tigris River that had been destroyed during the devastating air war. "Why did the Americans bomb it? Why did the British bomb it?" George asked.

I muttered a noncommittal reply. It was February 27, 1991, and the Gulf War was in its last full day. A

British journalist, I was returning to the center of Baghdad from an electricity substation on the western outskirts of the capital. Like so many power plants in Iraq, it had been bombed to ruins by U.S. and allied forces.

We came to the wreckage of a second bridge and George repeated his question, his voice rising with what I took to be indignation. Again, I avoided a straight answer. Here I was in the dying hours of a war that Iraqi President Saddam Hussein had proclaimed the "Mother of All Battles" in which American soldiers would drown in rivers of their own blood. With the country bombed into a preindustrial state after just six weeks of conflict, culminating in 100 hours in one of the biggest ground offensives since World War Two, now did not seem the time for an outsider from one of the key allies in the war with Iraq to express an opinion.

Finally we reached the only bridge across the Tigris in downtown Baghdad that was still standing. "Look at the bridge! Look at the bridge!" George exclaimed, incredulous and angry. "Why didn't they bomb that one also? Why is it still standing? If they want to finish Saddam, why did they not bomb it? They are crazy."

The Iraqis are a taciturn people under Saddam Hussein. Cowed by his ruthless rule, they generally either tell foreigners what they know the authorities expect them to say or they keep their views to themselves. Many Iraqis, for example, are so frightened of Saddam's secret police that they are convinced the traffic lights in Baghdad have hidden microphones that can pick up their conversations while they wait in their cars at intersections. Both before and during the 1991 Gulf War, silence from ordinary Iraqis often spoke louder than words.

George's forthright opinions thus came as a surprise. They were not, however, untypical of the moment, as Iraqis dared to ask why Saddam had led them on a disastrous adventure into Kuwait and why the international coalition brought together under United Nations auspices to end the Iraqi occupation had not gone a step further and ended Saddam's rule. They are questions that persist to this day and go to the heart of the debate over another U.S.-led war with Iraq, this time to oust Saddam.

As I entered Iraq from Jordan at a desolate customs post at Trebiel to cover the closing stages of the war, Saddam spoke on Baghdad radio to announce that his forces were "withdrawing" from Kuwait. It was, as shown by the bitter expressions on the drawn faces of silent soldiers and civilians on that cold morning, an admission of defeat dressed up as a declaration of triumph. "Applaud your victory, my dear citizens. You have faced 30 countries and the evil they have brought here," Saddam proclaimed. "In this mother of all battles we have succeeded in harvesting what we have sown." According to U.S. estimates given soon after the conflict, more than 100,000 Iraqi soldiers were killed and 300,000 wounded in the uneven contest that pitted Iraq's armed forces against the coalition of 28 Western, Arab and Muslim countries

THE GULF WAR

In response to the invasion of Kuwait by Iraq on August 2, 1990, a coalition of countries massed their armed forces in Saudi Arabia under the authority of the United Nations

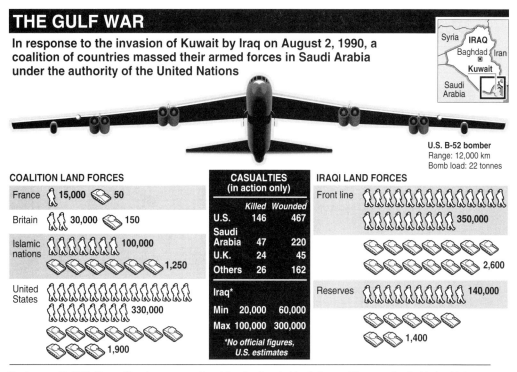

U.S. B-52 bomber
Range: 12,000 km
Bomb load: 22 tonnes

COALITION LAND FORCES

France   15,000   50

Britain   30,000   150

Islamic nations   100,000   1,250

United States   330,000   1,900

CASUALTIES (in action only)		
	Killed	Wounded
U.S.	146	467
Saudi Arabia	47	220
U.K.	24	45
Others	26	162
Iraq*		
Min	20,000	60,000
Max	100,000	300,000
*No official figures, U.S. estimates		

IRAQI LAND FORCES

Front line   350,000   2,600

Reserves   140,000   1,400

On January 17, 1991, the coalition began a massive air bombardment of Iraq's forces. After a month of raids, in which more bombs were dropped than in the whole of World War Two, there followed a ground offensive on February 24. In just 100 hours, Saddam Hussein's army was defeated and Kuwait liberated

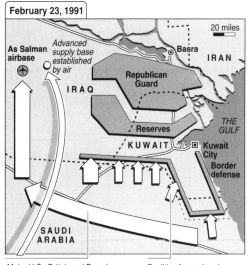

Major U.S., British and French forces make secret flanking move on February 23

Coalition forces break through border trenches using armored bulldozers

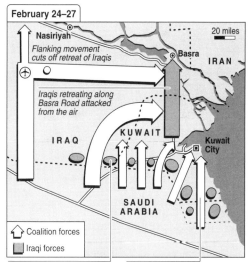

Thousands of Iraqi soldiers surrender as they are overrun

Islamic forces and U.S. Marines enter Kuwait City

Anti-aircraft fire and tracer flares light up the sky above Baghdad as U.S. and allied planes launch bombing raids at the start of the Gulf War, January 17, 1991. REUTERS

that President George Bush marshaled for the campaign. The United States, by contrast, lost fewer than 300 of its military, half of them in accidents and other incidents unrelated to combat.

Iraq had long harbored claims to Kuwaiti territory, and when Kuwait gained independence from Britain in 1961, British and Arab League troops were sent to the emirate to deter Iraqi expansionism. Rather than territorial ambition, however, the catalyst for Saddam's invasion in 1990 appears to have been a mix of economic pressures and a belief that the United States was engaged in a conspiracy to bring him down. A chilling indication of where that would lead came on July 17, 1990, in a speech by Saddam marking the 22nd anniversary of the coup that brought his Baath Party to power. He used it to launch an unprecedented verbal attack on his Gulf Arab neighbors, Kuwait and the United Arab Emirates, for producing far above their OPEC quotas in what he termed an American plot to drive down oil prices and thus deplete the revenues a heavily indebted Iraq needed to rebuild an economy shattered by eight years of war with Iran.

Saddam accused some Gulf states, creditors who bankrolled his conflict with Iran, of stabbing Iraq in the back "with a poisoned dagger" and warned them: "If words fail to protect Iraqis, something effective must be done to return things to their natural course and return usurped rights to their owners." He also accused Kuwait of stealing Iraqi crude from the Rumeila oilfield, revived Iraq's claims to Kuwaiti territory and underpinned his bellicose rhetoric by sending thousands of troops to the border. The United States, already increasingly at odds with Saddam over the acceleration of his attempts to develop nuclear and chemical weapons, responded by scheduling military exercises involving warships and aircraft in the Gulf. Even so, there was little sense among diplomats that war was on the horizon. In remarks that summed up the prevailing mood and subsequently were to prove so wide of the mark, the U.N. Secretary-General Javier Perez de Cuellar ventured this opinion on July 24: "I don't see either the Iraqis embarking on any military offensive against Kuwait, nor the Americans intervening in Middle East affairs." By August 2, Iraqi troops were in Kuwait City.

The Push into Kuwait

Did Saddam, in sending units of his million-man army into the tiny sheikhdom of Kuwait, misjudge the international outrage it would unleash? Or did Bush, still believing he could talk to a man the United States had done business with for years, misread the Iraqi leader's intentions? Either way, there were mixed messages. At a now legendary meeting in Baghdad on July 25 between Saddam and U.S. Ambassador April Glaspie, Saddam appears to have understood that Washington would not intervene in his dispute with Kuwait and to have taken that as a "green light" to start the tanks rolling south. Glaspie appears to have understood, and relayed back to the State Department, that Saddam would not use military muscle to get his way.

The invasion, branded "naked aggression" by a shocked Bush, challenged the New World Order that the U.S. president saw on the horizon in the heady months that followed the whirlwind collapse of Communism in Eastern Europe and the beginning of the end of more than four decades of Cold War. As Iraqi forces sped through Kuwait's southern oil fields toward the border with Saudi Arabia, it also became a growing menace to Washington's primary ally in the Gulf, to other Arab states and to the free flow of oil to the developed world. On August 6, by a vote of 13–0 that put the Soviet Union and China on the same side of the fence as the United States, the United Nations Security Council imposed some of the toughest economic sanctions in U.N. history on Iraq, ordering an arms embargo and a ban on its oil exports. Two days later, with the first U.S. military deployments to Saudi Arabia under way at the start of Operation Desert Shield, Saddam responded by annexing Kuwait. It was the start of a spiral of "who blinks first" moves that was to lead inexorably to war. But first the

President George Bush (left), Vice President Dan Quayle, Secretary of State
James Baker and Chief of Staff John Sununu walk toward the Oval Office of the
White House, February 23, 1991. President Bush returned from Camp David to
announce the beginning of the ground attack against Iraqi forces. REUTERS

world had to confront another, sinister drama that was to cement
Saddam's image in the West as a callous and calculating dictator.

Five-year-old Stuart Lockwood, a British boy caught up in Kuwait
by the Iraqi invasion, was among 13,000 Westerners detained in Iraq
and Kuwait in the unfolding conflict. On August 23, young Stuart
became a pawn in Saddam's game of blink when he appeared on
Baghdad television at a meeting with the Iraqi leader with around two
dozen British hostages, or as Saddam put it, "guests serving the cause

U.S. politician Jesse Jackson carries five-year-old Stuart Lockwood down the steps of an Iraqi aircraft which arrived at London's Heathrow airport carrying 200 hostages from Baghdad, September 2, 1990. Television footage of Lockwood, caught up in the Iraqi invasion of Kuwait, standing beside President Saddam Hussein was broadcast around the world. REUTERS

of peace." Clearly terrified as Saddam beckoned him forward, he clutched at the sides of his blue shorts. Then Saddam tousled his hair. "Are you getting your milk, Stuart, and cornflakes too?" Saddam asked the boy through a translator. The boy nodded.

If the gesture, broadcast around the world by CNN, was meant to show a human side to Saddam and portray him as a caring family man, it proved a massive miscalculation. Margaret Thatcher, the British prime minister, called it a "repulsive charade." As propaganda ploys go, it was crude in the extreme, though Saddam was to use similar means again to equally sickening effect in the world beyond Iraq's borders when he had captured American and allied pilots, cowed and bearing facial injuries sustained in ejecting from their aircraft and in beatings by their captors, paraded on television during the war.

Stuart Lockwood was among some 200 Western women and children released by Saddam in early September on a mercy flight negotiated by the Reverend Jesse Jackson, one of a succession of Western politicians who braved stiff criticism at home to journey to Baghdad over the weeks of the hostage crisis to plead for the freeing of the Iraqi president's "guests." The boy's father, Derek, had to stay behind. And, of the thousands held hostage, some 700 were moved to secret locations—vital installations including sensitive weapons development sites—as human shields against attack. The tactic, which Saddam ultimately abandoned in early December with the freeing of all international hostages, was later copied by Bosnian Serb forces using U.N. peacekeepers in a futile attempt to ward off NATO air strikes.

I arrived in Baghdad in early October to cover the hostage crisis and the drift toward war, flying in from Amman on one of the Iraqi Airways planes that were still defiantly plying the only air route open to Iraq. By then, Iraq was under a stringent embargo and subject to naval and air blockade. The United States had begun calling up reservists for the first time since the Vietnam War. And Saddam, the secular leader of a country famed for its beer and the nightspots of its vibrant capital of One Thousand and One Nights, had started playing the Islamic card. He had declared a "jihad," or holy war, against the United States and Israel and was exploiting the Israeli occupation of the West Bank and Gaza Strip to link the Palestinian cause to his own and rail at U.N. "double standards" over the occupation of Kuwait. But

Gulf War Chronology

1990

Aug 2   Iraq invades Kuwait at 2 a.m. (2300 GMT Aug 1). Emir flees to Saudi Arabia. United Nations Security Council condemns Iraqi occupation 14–0 and demands Baghdad withdraw.

Aug 6   Security Council agrees 13–0 to ban trade with Iraq except for medicine and some food for humanitarian relief.

Aug 7   President George Bush orders U.S. forces to Saudi Arabia.

Aug 8   Iraq annexes Kuwait.

Aug 16   Iraq orders 4,000 Britons and 2,500 Americans in Kuwait to report to hotels or be rounded up. Later says it will hold Westerners as human shields against attack.

Nov 29   U.N. Security Council votes 12–2 (Yemen and Cuba opposing) with one abstention (China) to authorize use of force against Iraq unless it withdraws from Kuwait by January 15.

Dec 6   President Saddam Hussein orders release of all foreign hostages.

1991

Jan 9   Iraqi Foreign Minister Tareq Aziz meets U.S. Secretary of State James Baker in a bid to avert war six days before a United Nations resolution authorizing force to drive Iraq from Kuwait takes effect. Baker fails to persuade Iraq to withdraw, saying, "Regrettably, ladies and gentlemen, in over six hours I heard nothing that suggested to me any Iraqi flexibility whatsoever."

Jan 17   U.S.-led allied forces start Gulf War by launching air and missile offensive against Iraqi positions and installations in Iraq and occupied Kuwait.

Jan 18 Iraq fires at least eight missiles at Israel in a bid to drag it into the conflict.

Jan 29 British forces commander says allies have destroyed 75 to 80 percent of Iraq's oil refining capacity.

Feb 8 U.S. says allied bombing wiped out one-eighth of Iraqi tanks and artillery in first 22 days of war.

Feb 13 U.S. bombs hit Baghdad shelter which Washington calls military bunker. Iraq says more than 300 civilians killed.

Feb 24 Ground war begins with allied night attack. U.S. General Norman Schwarzkopf says only light opposition. More than 14,000 Iraqis captured in first 24 hours of fighting.

Feb 26 Occupation of Kuwait ends when allied forces enter Kuwait City after lightning advance.

Feb 28 U.S. and allied forces cease fire at 8 a.m. Kuwait time—0500 GMT. Iraq tells army to stop fighting. Baghdad Radio insists Iraq won the war.

it was the human aspects that drew me into the story, my first encounter as a journalist with the Arab world and with a conflict of this magnitude.

Fatalistic Despair

Among the Westerners and Japanese still prevented from leaving Iraq, the mood that prevailed was almost one of fatalistic despair. At the al-Rashid, a concrete, marble and glass hotel built to withstand missile attacks, men constrained to enforced idleness would sit all day at the bar, drinking and bemoaning their lot. Occasionally, one would sob quietly or pick a fight when the strain of uncertainty and separation from loved ones became too great. "Sometimes...men break down and weep," Bertel Berg, a Swedish doctor among the hostages who passed his time counseling his fellows, told me. "The tears simply run. I tell them, 'Yes, I do that too,'" he said.

At the British embassy, men moved up by the Iraqis from Kuwait camped in the grounds and lined up at a courtesy telephone to stay in touch with home. I overheard one ask his wife why she was leaving him. At night, Western nurses and construction workers who had flocked to

United States Chairman of the Joint Chiefs of Staff Colin Powell and General Norman Schwarzkopf, Commander of the Allied Forces for Operation Desert Storm, in Riyadh, February 8, 1991. REUTERS

Baghdad on hefty salaries paid out by foreign contractors partied in clubs on vast quantities of alcohol and frequently paired up in grim, bacchanalian abandon.

"'We are all going to be dead' is a common phrase that seems to reflect the tensions behind the calm face foreigners put on their knife-edge existence between hope and despair," I wrote in one of my dispatches.

Among Iraqis, the mood was harder to gauge. The "minders" saw to that. Officially, the Iraqi Information Ministry provided all visiting foreign journalists with a ministry escort to assist with interviews, translate from Arabic if needed and help them avoid potential trouble on the streets. In reality, these escorts were intelligence officers there to keep watch on you, report back on any potentially damaging stories you were pursuing and make sure Iraqis parroted the party line. Usually sporting Saddam-style moustaches and often wearing wristwatches with a picture of Saddam's face on the dial, they would stand next to you as you interviewed Iraqis on the street and occasionally tell you not to ask certain questions. My "minder" provided an additional service free of charge. When translating from Arabic, he would sometimes elaborate on the answers.

This dawned on me during a visit to a school in Baghdad to see how a class of 26 seven-year-olds was living through the crisis. The entire class, schooled in Baghdad's view of events, sprang to its feet as we entered the room and chanted, "Long live our leader Saddam!" They added the refrain "Victory will be ours!" when they sat back down.

Children, though, are not generally chatty with strangers. Most of the students provided shy one-sentence answers to my translated questions, yet their responses were conveyed to me at great length. It was possible, however, to slip the "minders" on occasion—on evening visits to the restaurants that line the Tigris to eat barbecued Mazgouf, a delicate, flat river fish, at times when the ministry escort was occupied with another journalist, or in furtive conversations with one's driver in the privacy of a car speeding through Baghdad when the Information Ministry would suddenly order every journalist it could find lurking at the Rashid Hotel to rush off to an organized news conference or another "media opportunity." Such occasions, though rare, offered a keyhole into a different Iraq from the officially portrayed land of 17 million happy citizens delighted that Kuwait was now their country's 19th province and prepared to fight to the death for Saddam.

That insight emerged for me in the black humor, so often a barometer of suppressed discontent in a repressive state, which surfaced when sanctions began to bite. Iraq has the world's second largest proven oil reserves, yet by late October the embargo had halted the supply of the chemicals and additives needed to refine crude into gasoline and forced the introduction of petrol rationing. "This is what we got for invading Kuwait. Think what it will be like when we invade Israel," one man told me with a bitter smile as he drew his weekly ration at a filling station.

It was also possible to cut through the propaganda by ignoring it and reporting what you saw. One day, foreign journalists were invited to attend a parade in downtown Baghdad by members of the Popular Army, a volunteer reserve force that Iraq had touted as a formidable addition to its standing armed forces. "One million," came the reply when I asked one of our "minders" how many people would be marching in the parade. So my American colleague Jacki Lyden of National Public Radio and I set about counting the marchers as they filed past six abreast along the capital's Palestine Avenue, some with rifles, others with pitchforks, clubs or swords and yet others with no weapon at all. After discounting the rag-tag warriors we recognized as having marched past us at least twice, we decided our best estimate was 11,000.

By the end of 1990, the United Nations Security Council, by a vote of 12–2 with China abstaining, had passed its first resolution for 40 years authorizing the use of force against a member state and given

U.S. Army soldiers walk past tanks, some 30 miles from the Iraqi border, November 16, 1998. REUTERS

Iraq until January 15, 1991, to withdraw from Kuwait or face military action. Close to half a million troops from an astounding and erstwhile unlikely array of nations that grouped the United States and Syria in the same coalition had massed in Saudi Arabia and other areas of the Gulf ready to go to war. The number was to swell to roughly 660,000 troops by the time hostilities started. The foe that the coalition faced was, by most accounts, formidable, spearheaded by a Republican Guard hardened by eight years of apocalyptic conflict with Iran on terrain that came to resemble the killing fields of Flanders in World War One.

Breaking News

Iraq had the biggest standing army in the Middle East and was reported by the Pentagon to have deployed some 545,000 soldiers in or near Kuwait. It had not hesitated to use poison gas in the war with Iran and had turned chemical weapons against its own people, notably in the Kurdish town of Halabja in 1988. Saddam had also admitted to possessing binary chemical weapons and the means to deliver them, threatening to use them to "burn half of Israel." There was talk of towering, fortified sand berms on the border between Iraqi-occupied Kuwait and Saudi Arabia that the Iraqis would use to blunt any allied advance and of a sophisticated umbrella of radar and anti–aircraft defenses to check an assault from the air. The reality proved very different when the first war ever to be brought live from both sides onto the television screens of viewers around the world erupted shortly before 3 a.m. Baghdad time on Thursday, January 17.

President Bush spoke to Americans two hours after wave after wave of allied aircraft and Tomahawk cruise missiles opened Operation

White House Announces the Start of the Gulf War

WASHINGTON, Jan. 16, 1991 (Reuters)—The following is the text of White House spokesman Marlin Fitzwater's announcement of the start of the Gulf War:

"The liberation of Kuwait has begun.

"In conjunction with the forces of our coalition partners, the United States has moved under the code name Operation Desert Storm to enforce the mandates of the United Nations Security Council.

"As of 7 o'clock p.m. Eastern Standard Time (midnight GMT), Operation Desert Storm forces were engaging targets in Kuwait and Iraq. President Bush will address the nation at 9 o'clock p.m. tonight from the Oval Office. We will try to get you more as soon as we can.

"Thank you very much."

Desert Storm with a crippling bombardment of Iraqi airfields, Scud missile bases, command and control centers and communications links. "Tonight the battle has been joined," Bush declared in a televised address. "Our objectives are clear," Bush said. "Saddam Hussein's forces will leave Kuwait." But he also went beyond that. "We are determined to knock out Saddam Hussein's nuclear bomb potential. We will also destroy his chemical weapons facilities. Much of Saddam's artillery and tanks will be destroyed."

By the end of the war, allied aircraft had flown a staggering 116,000 combat sorties for the loss of 75 aircraft, 42 of them in combat and none in air-to-air engagements. Iraq, according to U.S. military estimates, lost 110 aircraft in the air and on the ground, a little under half its air force, and around 80 percent of its battle tanks, armored vehicles and artillery pieces.

Former British Prime Minister John Major rides on a tank while visiting British troops, January 8, 1991. Riding with him is Brigadier Christopher Hammerbeck. REUTERS

In the Reuters office in Baghdad, my colleague Maamoun Youssef experienced the opening minutes of the coalition blitz crouching beneath a table and dictating to his editors over a crackling telephone line until it suddenly went dead. The news ticker that slowly churned out our stories in the office also stuttered to a halt, ironically a few paragraphs into a story filed from aboard the *USS Wisconsin*. "Should war break out in the Gulf, a petty officer on this World War Two vintage battleship will be among the first to launch high-tech cruise missiles against Iraq," its opening sentence read. While Maamoun and the rest of Baghdad sheltered in homes in darkness inflicted by strikes on the city's power plants, residents of cities like Washington and London were able to watch the very same strikes on their television screens through a misty greenish haze engendered by the night-vision cameras that CNN and other broadcasters used to film the attacks from the relative safety of an upper floor of the Rashid Hotel.

The march of technology had yielded the computer-guided missiles that the United States and its allies were able to program, at times with pinpoint accuracy and at times not, to knock out specific targets. Having built much of Iraq's infrastructure during the lucrative years of cooperation with Saddam, the West was essentially able to destroy it using the construction blueprints to tell its "smart bombs" where to hit. Technology, though, had also given the world's media satellite telephones, portable television cameras and laptop computers that allowed journalists to file their reports and images from remote locations and independently of a nation's or army's communications systems.

The Gulf War was the first major conflict to put that technology into effect, and its use posed a challenge to both sides. In essence, they both sought to control the flow of news so as to paint their actions in the best possible light. In Baghdad, Iraqi minders insisted on listening in as broadcast journalists spoke to their anchors and censoring the stories that print reporters tapped out on their laptops before dictating over their satellite phones. In Saudi Arabia, journalists attached to U.S. and British ground forces and located at desert air bases as "pool reporters" were told by public affairs officers when they could use their satellite phones and given only limited access to troops. I was among a smaller group of journalists who would ignore the pools and set out each day from the dusty town of Hafr al Batin to hunt for news at the

Israeli soldiers stand inside a crater made when an Iraqi Scud missile exploded near an Arab village in the West Bank, January 29, 1991. REUTERS

border with Kuwait from obliging Egyptian forces, dodging patrols by units from the major contributor nations to the coalition. The approach yielded a very different picture of the battle readiness and morale among Iraqi forces from the one painted by the coalition's military briefers and the commander of U.S. forces in the Gulf, Vietnam veteran General H. "Stormin" Norman Schwarzkopf.

"Bomb, Bomb, Bomb"

Less than four weeks into the air war, we reported that Iraqi soldiers were deserting in droves, some crawling on their bellies through minefields to escape incessant bombing and starvation rations and surrender to coalition troops. "Every night it is bomb, bomb, bomb," one of the deserters told me. "In Iran, it was army against army. Here, we've seen only bombs."

We also reported that Iraqi forces had begun to abandon forward positions on the southern Kuwaiti border. "The bombing was so heavy that we think they left," one allied officer remarked. Soon after, I drove through the night to Dhahran, Saudi Arabia, to prepare to leave for Baghdad. As I pressed on south, convoy after convoy of U.S. military vehicles passed me heading north on a road that leads to the border with Kuwait and then forks off toward the frontier with Iraq. It struck me that all the vehicles in the convoys, ferrying munitions, supplies and tanks on flatbed trucks to the front, had their headlights blazing. Only a military confident that it has total air supremacy does that. The ground offensive was about to start.

Iraq could claim only one victory of sorts on the ground, an incursion into the Saudi Arabian coastal town of Khafji at the end of January. An Iraqi raiding force held on for two days before it was beaten back by Saudi troops. The incursion also yielded the Iraqis their first woman prisoner of war, Army Specialist Melissa Rathbun-Nealy, a 21-year-old driver from Grand Rapids, Michigan, who strayed into the fighting and fell into Iraqi hands when her transport truck got stuck in the sand.

A Glimpse of Truth Under American Bombs

Bernd Debusmann

The scene remains etched in my memory: in the air raid shelter of Baghdad's Rashid hotel, Iraqi government officials, residents of the area around the hotel, and a few foreign journalists and diplomats settle in for another uncomfortable night of sleeping on the floor, much too close for comfort in the dense air thrown up by sweat and fear and too many people in too small an area. But who would complain? The shelter, Iraqi officials asserted, was built to withstand even nuclear blasts.

Those in the room, perhaps 150, knew from the first night of the bombing, January 17, 1991, that the shelter was deep enough to block out the crash of high explosives outside but not deep enough to prevent the ground from moving, as in a small earthquake. You felt some of the bombs that knocked out the power plant, the telephone exchanges, the municipal water plants, the airport. But you didn't hear them.

The emergency generator of the Rashid, Baghdad's flagship hotel, provided enough power to light the stairs to the elevators but not the elevators themselves. There was enough power for dim emergency bulbs in the shelter. And there was enough power to run a television set.

When it flickered into action, it showed a quartet of pilots in flight overalls singing patriotic songs in praise of the great motherland. Then someone turned up the volume and Saddam Hussein, looking drawn and tense, began to address a people who had emerged from their houses and air raid shelters that morning in dazed disbelief at the ferocity of the opening salvo in the war.

Within minutes of the first missile slamming into Baghdad, the lights went out in the ancient capital. The telephones went dead all over the country. Toilets stopped flushing. The damage was greater than all the damage Iraq had suffered from Iranian missile attacks in the eight years of the Iran–Iraq war.

On the television screen, Saddam told his country that the imperialist aggression had begun but that Iraq would emerge triumphant, by the will of God and despite the Americans' superior technology. In the air raid shelter, no one paid attention. And some of those sitting closest to the screen turned their back on it. Nothing out of the ordinary anywhere else. A flash of truth in Iraq, where the personality of Saddam was all-pervasive and where even mild expressions of discontent could draw brutal punishment.

In conversations in the first few days of the bombing, it became clear that Iraqis viewed their government propaganda with deep cynicism. In Iraq's climate of fear, they did not criticize openly—there might always be an informer around. Distance from the leadership came through nevertheless. "We will surely triumph over the evil forces and we will liberate Palestine," one man told me, borrowing the words from a Saddam speech. He then paused, ever so slightly, and added: "Even if we have to live underground while we do it."

In the runup to what might be a second U.S. war against Iraq, some of the debate on the rights, wrongs or reasons centered on "unfinished business," or

Amar Adnan, who lost his seven-member family when a U.S. bomb punched into a Baghdad shelter in the Gulf War, celebrates his birthday inside the shelter, January 10, 2001. Washington said the target was a military bunker, the Iraqi government said more than 300 civilians lost their lives in the attack. REUTERS

(continued)

the legacy left by one President Bush for the next, his son. How close did the United States come to finishing the business in 1991? Very close. In a society built on power and fear, every air raid that blew apart a bridge, destroyed a building and prompted an air raid alarm—often long after the missiles or bombs had struck—stripped away a piece of credibility from the leadership.

At least in the first three weeks of the bombing campaign, the popular wisdom that people under enemy bombardment rally behind their leaders did not appear to apply to Iraq. That may have changed after U.S. missiles slammed into a crowded air raid shelter in Baghdad's Amariya district on February 13 and killed hundreds of those sheltering inside, including women and children. Washington called the shelter a military command center. The Iraqis said at least 300 civilians were killed.

But if support for the regime trickled away in night after night of air raids, it faced its greatest danger after the end of the tank-and-infantry war that followed the air campaign. With the Iraqi armed forces, the world's fourth-largest at the beginning of the war, cut to shreds, forced into surrender and driven from Kuwait, autonomy-seeking Kurds in the north and dissident Shi'ite Moslems in the south rose in rebellion.

In broadcasts on opposition radio stations and the Voice of America, U.S. leaders including President Bush had urged popular revolt. When it happened, the United States stood back. At the height of the twin revolts, anti-Saddam forces controlled most of Iraq's territory and fought within an hour's drive from his capital. Basra, Iraq's second city, was in the hands of Shi'ite rebels.

Then Saddam struck back, using helicopter gunships, tanks and artillery to cut the dissidents to pieces. Iraqis fleeing the south to U.S.-controlled areas reported that Saddam's counterattacking loyalists had hanged dissidents from the barrels of tanks and lampposts. Some of the fighting in the south took place literally under the eyes of American troops. Their orders: don't interfere, your mission was to liberate Kuwait, and it is over.

During weeks of travel in Baghdad and southern Iraq a year after the beginning of the war, at a time when trade sanctions had begun to bite deeply, one of many conspiracy theories—voiced even by educated Iraqis—held that Saddam and Bush had actually acted in concert to lure dissidents in the north and south into the open and then destroy them. In sharp contrast to disenchantment with Saddam in the bombing phase of the war, the most widely held view a year later was of President Bush as an evil, heartless schemer out to starve the Iraqi people and deny their children medicines.

Such views were reinforced partly by constant repetition, partly by television clips that borrowed Madison Avenue techniques. One sticks in mind: a documentary called The File, which began airing on the first anniversary of the beginning of the war. Sandwiched between shots of the White House, cruise missiles taking off for targets in Iraq, devastated power stations, broken bridges and ruined houses, there was a nine-second clip featuring President Bush. His soundbite became so familiar it needed no Arabic subtitles.

"Let me also make clear that the United States has no quarrel with the Iraqi people," Bush said. Cut. Switch to an emaciated baby, eyes too large for its shrunken face. Cut. Switch to a sobbing mother at the funeral of her child. Cut. Switch to a grizzled old man in front of the charred ruins of what used to be his house.

The chief villain, in the eyes of many, was President Bush, whom Saddam took to calling a "poisonous snake" and "despicable dwarf." More than a decade later, Saddam described another U.S. president as "wicked Bush" and "little Bush." A family affair.

The capture of allied servicemen and women by Iraq gave armchair viewers of the conflict a sense that there was more to war than television images of slow-flying cruise missiles passing through Baghdad and Pentagon-supplied footage of bombs hitting their targets. What drove it home in horrific fashion, and delivered Saddam his biggest propaganda coup of the war, was the nighttime bombing on February 13 of what Iraq called a residential bomb shelter in the middle-class Baghdad suburb of Amariya and what the United States called an Iraqi command and communications bunker. According to Iraq, more than 300 civilians, many of them women and children, were killed when two precision bombs pierced the structure's hardened

The coastline of Saudi Arabia near the Kuwait border is soaked with oil, January 26, 1991. Iraq opened the taps of Kuwaiti oil terminals during the Gulf War, causing a massive oil slick. REUTERS

concrete shell and exploded inside. Washington suggested Saddam had deliberately placed civilians at the site to spare it from attack. Yet Western reporters who went to the scene said they saw no evidence that the facility was used for military purposes.

"I obviously don't have access to the kind of intelligence information that the Americans have. All I have is the evidence of my own eyes. What I saw there were women and children dead, some burnt beyond recognition," British Broadcasting Corporation correspondent Jeremy Bowen reported.

Saddam had made himself popular among many ordinary Arabs by portraying the conflict as a battle between the Arab people and an unholy alliance of infidel Americans, Arab traitors and Zionists. When he launched Scud missile attacks on Israel, some Palestinians living under Israeli occupation in the West Bank and Gaza Strip danced on their rooftops. The Amariya bombing only deepened popular hostility to the Gulf War in the Middle East. It raised questions about whether the United States was exceeding the mandate from the United Nations to use "all necessary means" to end Iraq's occupation of Kuwait. And it

Iraqi armor destroyed during the Gulf War at a site inside Kuwait and 35 miles south of the Iraqi border, November 15, 1998. REUTERS

Surrendering Iraqi soldiers walk to a U.S. position, March 19, 1991. REUTERS

punctured the myth that "smart" bombs spare civilian lives. They can be wrongly targeted, based on inadequate intelligence as with the Amariya attack, or they may not be "smart" at all. Only around 5 percent of the bombs rained on Iraq and on Iraqi positions in Kuwait during the Gulf War were advanced enough to be termed "smart," according to some estimates. The rest were conventional bombs deployed at times with less than pinpoint accuracy and the inevitable "collateral damage"—military speak for civilian casualties.

Saddam brought more medieval means to the conflict than "smart" bombs. Though he did not unleash his chemical weapons or biological agents, he engaged in environmental warfare, setting fire to Kuwaiti oil fields and spilling an estimated 1.5 million barrels of crude into the Gulf. Oil, the black gold of prosperity for Iraq and its Gulf Arab neighbors, had literally been turned into a weapon to destroy Kuwait. Yet with his cards running out, Saddam was already suing for a negotiated peace under Soviet auspices. On February 22, Day 37 of the war, Bush followed his rejection of those overtures with a point-blank ultimatum to Saddam—withdraw unconditionally from Kuwait within 24 hours or face a ground war.

High Noon Deadline

At 4 a.m. Baghdad time on February 24, after Saddam had ignored Bush's "high noon" deadline, Schwarzkopf sent allied forces storming into Kuwait and Iraq in one of the biggest ground invasions since the D-Day landings in France in 1944. Around 10,000 Iraqi soldiers, exhausted and frightened, surrendered in the initial hours of the onslaught.

A U.S. Marine searches an Iraqi prisoner of war at a holding area, January 19, 1991. The prisoners were taken after the Marines attacked oil platforms occupied by the Iraqis off the Kuwaiti coast. REUTERS

"The liberation of Kuwait has now entered its final phase," Bush declared. "I have complete confidence in the ability of the coalition forces swiftly and decisively to accomplish their mission."

My colleague Peter Bale rode into a devastated Kuwait City on February 27 with Kuwaiti troops to witness the liberation of the capital. "On the final drive, pockets of Iraqi soldiers crouched beside the road, guarded by American and Kuwaiti troops, as our column of tanks and armored vehicles swept by like a carnival parade," Bale reported of the ride into the city on the heels of the Iraqi retreat.

Elsewhere in the theater of a war that had become a rout, a far grimmer business was under way. On the road leading north from

Kuwait City inhabitants look at the dead body of an Iraqi soldier in Kuwait City after the withdrawal of the Iraqi army from Kuwait, February 27, 1991. REUTERS

Kuwait City toward Iraq, coalition aircraft pounded columns of retreating Iraqi troops and armor, killing a reported 10,000 Iraqis on a road that became known as the "Highway of Death." In southern Iraq west of the city of Basra, hundreds of tanks from the 1st and 3rd Armored divisions of the U.S. Army's VII Corps trapped the remnants of Saddam's vaunted Republican Guard and set about destroying it as an armored force in one of the biggest tank engagements since the Battle of the Bulge in World War Two.

Kuwaiti and Saudi soldiers dance as they arrive in Kuwait City after the withdrawal of the Iraqi army from Kuwait, February 27, 1991. REUTERS

Yet, having blocked off the Iraqi army's escape route, Desert Storm commander Schwarzkopf "opened the gate" and allowed surviving soldiers through toward Baghdad with their weapons after Bush ordered a ceasefire. "We were 150 miles away from Baghdad and there was nobody between us and Baghdad," Schwarzkopf said. "If it had been our intention to overrun the country, we could have done it unopposed."

The question of why U.S. forces did not push all the way north to Baghdad remains contentious to this day. Certainly, had they done so, Bush senior would not have retained the support of Arab and other Muslim allies in the coalition he built around a United Nations mandate to end the occupation of one sovereign country by another. Yet the decision also allowed Saddam to use the vestiges of his shattered army to crush uprisings by Shi'ite Muslims in southern Iraq and Iraqi Kurds in the north that followed the end of the Gulf War. Arguably, the risk of a chastened Saddam was more palatable to the United States and its allies among Iraq's neighbors than a splintered Iraq whose implosion might have unleashed a violent redrafting of the region's borders.

On the day George Bush senior declared the start of the Gulf War, he quoted a simple American soldier, Master Sergeant J.P. Kendall, in explaining the rationale behind the attack on Iraq. "We're here for more than just the price of a gallon of gas," Bush quoted Kendall as saying. "What we're doing is going to chart the future of the world for the next 100 years. It's better to deal with this guy now than five years from now."

Eleven years on, those are words that must resonate with President George W. Bush as he contemplates his options for completing his father's unfinished business.

The Iran–Iraq War: Saddam's Regional Ambitions

Alistair Lyon

"I repeat that accepting this (resolution) was more deadly for me than taking poison."

Ayatollah Ruhollah Khomeini on accepting U.N. Security Council resolution 598 calling for a ceasefire and withdrawal of warring forces

"The General Command have decided to rearrange your defensive positions to the rear after your strong blows absorbed the advance of the enemy."

President Saddam Hussein to a retreating Iraqi Fourth Army Corps

As dusk fell, buses, cars and motorcycles jammed the exits from the vast Behesht-e Zahra cemetery outside Tehran. It was late on a Thursday, the favored weekly visiting day for the relatives of thousands upon thousands of Iranian war "martyrs" who rest here in tightly packed graves. Most mourners were on their way home, but as I wandered through this city of the dead, family groups loomed out of the gathering darkness as they tended the tombs of their loved ones, washing the gravestones with rosewater, strewing flowers, lighting candles and reciting prayers. Children, observing another cemetery tradition, handed out sweets to passersby. Youths on motorcycles belted out religious verses as they clattered down roads that criss-cross the sprawling grounds. Fading photographs of young men stared from countless glass boxes held in iron frames above gravestones that carried inscriptions describing how and where the occupants were killed.

Even before the Iran–Iraq war, the cemetery held a special place in the heart of the late Ayatollah Ruhollah Khomeini because it was the burial place for many of those killed in the turmoil of the revolution he fathered. He made a point of visiting it soon after his triumphant return from exile in 1979 and vowed to turn it into a "city" of martyrs. He can hardly have guessed just how fast it would grow.

The cemetery is a grim reminder of the sacrifices Iranians made during the 1980–88 war with Saddam Hussein's Iraq. Upwards of a quarter of a million Iranian soldiers and civilians are thought to have perished in the conflict pitting two of the Middle East's biggest oil producers against each other. Iraq lost more than 100,000 soldiers dead, an even greater figure relative to its smaller population. The precise toll will probably never be known.

The late leader and founder of the Islamic revolution, Ayatollah Khomeini, speaks from a balcony of the Alavi school in Tehran during the country's revolution in February 1979. REUTERS

Members of the Iranian leadership, including President Mohammad Khatami (second right), former President Akbar Hashemi Rafsanjani (fourth right) and Ayatollah Khomeini's grandson Hasan Khomeini (fourth left), listen on June 4, 2001, to the Supreme Leader of the Islamic Revolution, Ayatollah Ali Khamenei, during a ceremony to mark the 12th anniversary of the death of Ayatollah Khomeini, June 3, 1989. REUTERS

The struggle, among one of the longest conventional wars of the 20th century, scarred both nations. Now, with war clouds again gathering over Iraq, memories of that ruinous contest are helping to shape Iranian attitudes toward U.S. threats to depose Saddam. President George W. Bush contends that "regime change" is the only way to ensure the Iraqi leader never uses weapons of mass destruction against the United States or its allies, either directly or by giving them to extremist groups. Iranians, with extensive first-hand experience of Iraqi poison gas attacks, recall bitterly that the United States lent ever-increasing support to the Iraqi war effort in the 1980s, when Washington viewed Tehran's Islamic revolutionary fervor as a greater evil than Iraq's aggressive posturing. The irony, in view of today's rhetoric from Washington, is that Saddam owes his survival in no small part to U.S. backing that lasted through the war until Iraq's 1990 invasion of Kuwait.

"I believe Iranians feel that any regime in Iraq would be better than Saddam's," Iranian Vice President Mohammad Ali Abtahi said in a Reuters interview. He noted Western tolerance of Saddam's past use of chemical weapons against Iran, now part of a crime catalog that Bush cites to demonize the Iraqi leader. "In those days, the West, because it was against Iran, gave Saddam the opportunity to use them," Abtahi said. "If they had confronted him then, we wouldn't be observing today's events."

But while debate rages in the West over the prospect of war, Iranians are torn between not-so-secret hopes that their archenemy will be removed and fears that their own country—lumped by Bush into an "axis of evil" with Iraq and North Korea—could be next up for "regime change" as part of the war on global terrorism that Bush declared after the September 11 attacks on the United States.

Tehran's View on the U.S.–Iraq Standoff

I had traveled to Tehran in the fall of 2002 and had the opportunity to witness first hand what Iranians were thinking, from the grieving families of the Iran–Iraq war dead to government officials in the corridors of power.

It was immediately clear that Iranian feelings toward the United States are complex and have certainly moved on from the hostility of the early days of the revolution. A debate was raging over the publication of the findings of two Iranian polling institutes that showed a majority of Iranians in favor of dialog with the United States, drawing the wrath of the conservative-dominated judiciary.

Yet memories linger of lavish U.S. support for the Shah during the Cold War and covert operations stretching back to the CIA-orchestrated overthrow of Iran's nationalist prime minister, Mohammad Mossadeq, and the restoration of Pahlavi rule in 1953.

Iranians have not forgotten the Carter administration's disastrous 1980 attempt at a military rescue of American embassy staff held hostage by Tehran students. Later on, the U.S. entanglement in secret arms-for-hostages deals in the mid-1980s, even though it worked to Iran's advantage, was not calculated to inspire Iranian confidence in the morality of U.S. foreign policy. And resentment still festers over the July 1988 downing of an Iranian airliner by a U.S. missile that killed 290 people—and helped convince Iran's leaders of the futility of pursuing war against an Iraq backed by both superpowers, the United States and what was then the Soviet Union.

The Iranian government describes its stance as one of "active neutrality." But this masks alarm about the upheaval that war between two of its bitterest foes may spark. The policy treads cautiously between bolder voices at each end of the Islamic republic's political spectrum. Anti-American conservatives say Iran should fight any U.S. attack on its Muslim neighbor. Radical reformers advocate unabashed cooperation with the United States to get rid of Saddam and reap postwar rewards. Iran's divided leadership hopes to neutralize the dangers posed by a

U.S.-led assault on Iraq without sacrificing the possible benefits of "regime change" next door—and without becoming a new target in America's war on terrorism. The influential Akbar Hashemi Rafsanjani, who when president kept Iran neutral in the 1990–91 Gulf crisis, compares a U.S. strike on Iraq to having "a python tackle a scorpion."

Officially, Tehran opposes any unilateral U.S. military action, while advising Iraq to avert regional chaos by obeying U.N. resolutions on disarmament. Foreign Ministry spokesman Hamid Reza Asefi told me that an invasion would stir more hatred of America in a Muslim world already angered by U.S. support for Israel. "We should let the Iraqi people determine their own destiny," he said. Asefi questioned whether Washington was really concerned about Iraq's quest for weapons of mass destruction. "Is this new information? Or did they know it 20 years ago when they equipped Iraq to attack Iran?" If Iraq came under U.S. attack, Iran would look to its own security interests, Asefi said. It would try to avoid any territorial disintegration of its ethnically and religiously diverse neighbor and head off any flood of refugees across its border.

Potential Gains

Among Iran's potential gains from an Iraqi defeat are the removal of Saddam and any banned weapons he may have. In addition, Tehran could hope for an end to any threat from the Mujahideen Khalq movement, which has several thousand Iranian opposition fighters based in Iraq and is sponsored by Saddam. However, a U.S. victory would fuel Iranian fears of encirclement.

Iranian policymakers worry about the unpredictable aftermath of a U.S. invasion. If the assault were a swift success, leading to a stable

Iraqi President Saddam Hussein practices launching a rocket-propelled grenade in this undated official Iraqi picture from the Iran–Iraq war. Official handout.

government in Baghdad, Iran would suddenly face a potent rival for Western investment in its energy sector. Its holy city of Qom would lose its temporary primacy as a seat of Shi'ite learning if religious scholars returned to Iraq's shrine cities of Najaf and Karbala. And any democratic flowering in Iraq would spur demands for faster reform of Iran's creaking system of clerical rule.

If, on the other hand, a U.S. attack went awry, Iran might find itself facing waves of refugees—and perhaps even a last-ditch salvo of poison gas missiles fired by a doomed Iraqi ruler bent on vengeance against his non-Arab foes. Should Iraq descend into civil war, any appeal from Iraqi Shi'ites would force Iran to weigh the domestic cost of ignoring their plight against the external risk inherent in an intervention that would horrify U.S. regional allies such as Sunni-ruled Saudi Arabia.

Nightmare scenarios aside, Iran could play a constructive role in a postwar Iraq, as it did in promoting a broad-based government in Afghanistan after the defeat of the Taliban. Iran's regional weight, along with its influence over Iraqi Shi'ites and Kurds, could help stabilize a post-Saddam Iraq.

There is quite clearly no love lost for the Iraqi leader in Iran. In October of 2002, thousands of people chanted "Death to Saddam" at a Tehran rally. The chants erupted during an address by Supreme Leader Ayatollah Ali Khamenei, even though he had not referred to the Iraq crisis.

The anti-Iraqi fervor conjured up memories of the end of the grinding Iran–Iraq war 14 years earlier when a mood of somberness and gloom had prevailed over Tehran. Iranians were shocked when Ayatollah Khomeini told them that for reasons of "expediency" and "the interest of the revolution" he was abandoning his previous uncompromising refusal to end the war. Iran had accepted U.N. Security Council resolution 598 calling for a ceasefire and withdrawal of warring forces at midnight on July 17, almost a year after the council had adopted it. "I repeat that accepting this (resolution) was more deadly for me than taking poison," the aged cleric declared. But few questioned his decision, and by the time the ceasefire took effect there was widespread relief in war-weary Iran, too, that the conflict, and the enormous sacrifices it had demanded, was finally over.

Iraqi women fighters march during a military parade to mark the anniversary of the end of the 1980–88 Iran–Iraq war in Baghdad, August 8, 2002. REUTERS

The scenes in Tehran at that time contrasted sharply with those in Baghdad. Ecstatic Iraqis took to the streets on August 20, 1988, the day the U.N. ceasefire came into effect. I had just arrived in the Iraqi capital to report the event, which to me hardly sounded like a ceasefire. Jubilant soldiers shot endless volleys from assault rifles and anti-aircraft guns into the night sky, heedless of the falling bullets, which inflicted scores of fatalities on Baghdad residents and smashed just about every car windshield in the city. Conscripts just back from the front were among those killed in this way. After years of tension, sadness and fear, people in the Iraqi capital could not contain their joy at the end of a nightmare their leader had set in motion eight years earlier. Yet Saddam, claiming a victory for all true Arabs, was the hero of the hour for the revelers who brandished his portrait as they danced.

It was not the war Saddam had in mind when his armored columns thrust across the border on September 22, 1980. He had envisaged a quick triumph over an enemy still in turmoil after the 1979 Islamic revolution. However, the invasion proved to be a rallying point for Iran's Shi'ite clerical leaders, who used it to unify the country and consolidate the revolution. Iran turned out to be a far more resilient foe than Saddam had anticipated. And in Khomeini, he found a stubborn adversary implacably opposed to the secular Arab nationalist model championed by the Iraqi leader.

Historic Arab–Persian and Sunni–Shi'ite rivalries helped set the stage for their clash, as did old territorial disputes and each country's ambitions to dominate the Gulf. But Saddam went to war because he spied an opportunity to weaken a regional rival and pre-empt Iran's declared goal of exporting its revolution to its next-door neighbor.

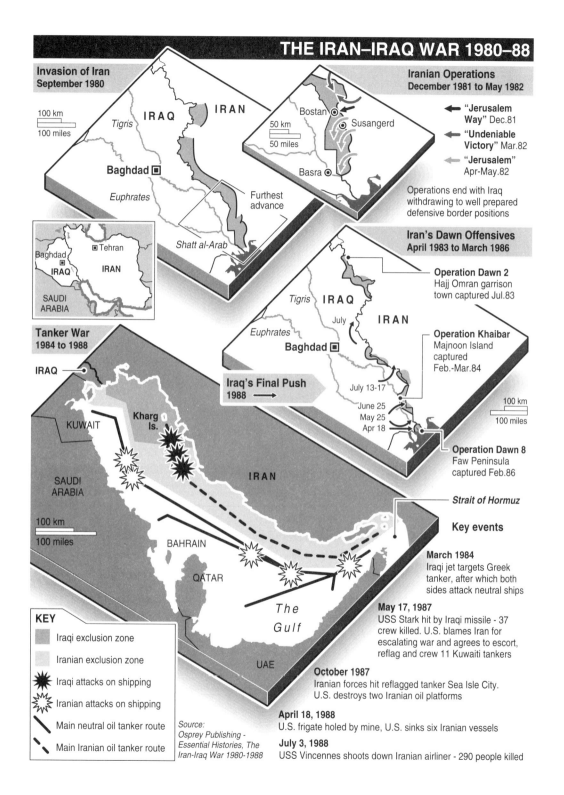

THE IRAN–IRAQ WAR 1980–88

Invasion of Iran
September 1980

100 km
100 miles

IRAQ   IRAN
Tigris
Baghdad ▣
Euphrates
Furthest advance
Shatt al-Arab

Tehran
Baghdad ▣
IRAQ   IRAN
SAUDI ARABIA

Iranian Operations
December 1981 to May 1982

50 km
50 miles

Bostan ◉
Susangerd ◉
Basra ◉

◀━ "Jerusalem Way" Dec.81
◀━ "Undeniable Victory" Mar.82
◀━ "Jerusalem" Apr-May.82

Operations end with Iraq withdrawing to well prepared defensive border positions

Iran's Dawn Offensives
April 1983 to March 1986

Tigris IRAQ
July
IRAN
Euphrates
Baghdad ▣

Iraq's Final Push
1988 ━▶

July 13-17
June 25
May 25
Apr 18

Operation Dawn 2
Hajj Omran garrison town captured Jul.83

Operation Khaibar
Majnoon Island captured Feb.-Mar.84

100 km
100 miles

Operation Dawn 8
Faw Peninsula captured Feb.86

Tanker War
1984 to 1988

IRAQ
KUWAIT
Kharg Is.
SAUDI ARABIA
IRAN
BAHRAIN
QATAR
The Gulf
UAE

100 km
100 miles

Strait of Hormuz

Key events

March 1984
Iraqi jet targets Greek tanker, after which both sides attack neutral ships

May 17, 1987
USS Stark hit by Iraqi missile - 37 crew killed. U.S. blames Iran for escalating war and agrees to escort, reflag and crew 11 Kuwaiti tankers

October 1987
Iranian forces hit reflagged tanker Sea Isle City. U.S. destroys two Iranian oil platforms

April 18, 1988
U.S. frigate holed by mine, U.S. sinks six Iranian vessels

July 3, 1988
USS Vincennes shoots down Iranian airliner - 290 people killed

KEY

▨ Iraqi exclusion zone
▨ Iranian exclusion zone
✸ Iraqi attacks on shipping
✸ Iranian attacks on shipping
━ Main neutral oil tanker route
╍ Main Iranian oil tanker route

Source: Osprey Publishing - Essential Histories, The Iran-Iraq War 1980-1988

119

Fear and Loathing

If fear helped start the war, loathing prolonged it. Saddam and Khomeini were locked into a bitter test of wills. It became a personal duel between two men imbued with a sense of destiny wrapped in incompatible world views—Khomeini's insistence on the supremacy of Islam over the state versus Saddam's determination to separate an all-powerful state from religion.

Saddam had assumed the presidency in July 1979, unceremoniously pushing his former mentor, President Ahmed Hassan al-Bakr, into "retirement." Even earlier, Saddam had wasted little time in grabbing the real levers of power after the 1968 coup that helped his Baathist party take over Iraq. He inserted party cells throughout the machinery of the state and society and subjugated the security services and armed forces to party control. After nationalizing Iraq's oil industry, Saddam used surging oil revenues in the 1970s to launch an impressive effort to build Iraq's military strength, develop nonconventional weapons and spur economic progress. He channeled development funds to the southern heartlands of Iraq's underprivileged Shi'ite majority, whose loyalties, like those of the Kurds in the north, he mistrusted. But Saddam also sought to crush religious opposition to the secular Baath party, based in the minority Sunni Muslim community.

Shi'ites accounted for about 60 percent of Iraq's 16 million people at the time, with half of the rest Sunni Arabs and half non-Arab Kurds, who were mainly Sunni. Saddam signed an autonomy agreement with the Kurds in 1970, but it remained largely a dead letter. Iraqi Kurdish guerrillas renewed their rebellion in 1974 and proved hard to suppress until Saddam signed the Algiers Accord with the Shah in 1975. The accord upheld Iran's demand for the Shatt al-Arab and other river borders to be demarcated along the thalweg, or deepest channel, and called on both sides to cease "all infiltrations of a subversive nature." The Shah then cut off aid to the Kurdish rebellion, which swiftly collapsed. Saddam thus made substantial gains from the Algiers Accord, but the territorial concession it had entailed annoyed him. The Shatt al-Arab was Iraq's main outlet to the Gulf, where it had only 19 miles of open coastline. Iraqi anxiety over this limited access fueled tension with Kuwait during and after the war with Iran.

Overthrow the Baathists, Khomeini Urged

Khomeini had openly urged Iraqis to overthrow their Baathist rulers in April 1980. As early Iranian efforts at counterrevolution died, along with American dreams of plucking the embassy hostages to safety, Saddam saw a chance to snuff out the threat of Iranian-inspired subversion and become the champion of Arab rulers quaking in fear of Khomeini. Saudi Arabia assured him of its support. At the time, the United States, European powers and the Soviet Union perceived revolutionary Iran as a far greater threat to regional stability and their own interests than secular Iraq, despite its leader's far-reaching ambitions. This unusual confluence of world opinion in the final years of the Cold War emboldened Saddam to go to war with his diplomatically isolated neighbor. The Iraqi leader was brimming with confidence in the ability of his Soviet-armed military machine to defeat Iran's supposedly much-weakened armed forces. He made a fatal error.

Ignoring the adage "never attack a revolution" was to prove a costly misjudgment. Iranians united behind their leaders. Many, such as those who joined the Basij volunteer militia, were willing to die for their country, Islam and Khomeini—as well as the promise of Paradise.

Iraqi prisoners of war form a line after being released at the Munthiriya border post with Iran, May 4, 2000. The POWs returned home to a hero's welcome almost 12 years after the end of the 1980–88 war. REUTERS

An Iranian businessman, who served in a front-line anti-aircraft unit during the war, recalled in late 2002 how truckloads of mostly teenaged Basij volunteers would arrive at the front. "They were given one or two days of military training, a key (to Paradise) to hang around their necks and a Koran. A few hours before an attack, a mullah would recite the Koran and they would chant slogans and Koranic verses until they had worked themselves almost into a trance. They would fight among themselves for the chance to walk over minefields. When they attacked, chanting Allahu Akbar (God is greatest) until the ground shook, the Iraqis would wet their pants, as we knew from those we captured."

On September 17, 1980, Saddam tore up the Algiers Accord on television. Five days later, his forces thrust into Iran, while Iraqi warplanes attacked Iranian airfields, military targets and oil installations. Saddam had planned a blitzkrieg modeled on Israel's swift victory in the 1967 Middle East war, with the declared aim of seizing the eastern half of the Shatt al-Arab and 190 square miles of disputed border territory. But military targets included Iran's oil-rich southwestern province of Khuzestan, populated partly by ethnic Arabs. And the underlying political objective was to prompt the collapse of Iran's clerical leadership.

Iraq made early gains, occupying the southern city of Khorramshahr and besieging Abadan in October. But Iran's U.S.-trained air force survived the initial Iraqi assaults and hit back, knocking out Iraq's oil exports from its southern fields for the duration of the war.

Appeals for a ceasefire from the United Nations, France, the Soviet Union and other parties fell on deaf ears. Saudi Arabia opened its oil taps to compensate for lost production from Iraq and Iran. Only a week after the outset of war, Iraq was inviting outside powers to mediate. Khomeini was in no mood to play. Far from suing for peace, he was bent on ejecting and punishing the invader in Allah's name.

Iran's officer corps had suffered purges of its pro-Shah officers, but Khomeini, capitalizing on his country's three-to-one population advantage over Iraq, was able to recruit many volunteers for the Revolutionary Guard and Basij militia. Iran began counteroffensives in January 1981, unleashing "human wave" assaults against the overstretched Iraqi forces.

Such fervor contrasted with the desertions and conscription evasion experienced by the Iraqi army. Saddam took charge of the war, overruling his cowed military planners. Iraqi leaders had assumed that ethnic Arabs in Iranian cities such as Khorramshahr and Abadan would welcome the invaders. In fact they fled the Iraqi advance. Conversely, Saddam could take comfort from the failure of Iraqi Shi'ites to heed Khomeini's calls for them to rise against him.

Stalemate

As the ground war settled into stalemate, Saddam sought to break the pattern with an offensive against the town of Susangerd in a central enclave in March 1981. It failed, and until the last year of the war the Iraqi army was to remain on the defensive. In September 1981 the Iranians broke the Iraqi siege of Abadan. After a big Iranian offensive in March 1982, which ended up two months later with an Iraqi withdrawal from Khorramshahr, Saddam set the new tone. "The General Command have decided to rearrange your defensive positions to the rear after your strong blows absorbed the advance of the enemy," he told the Iraqi Fourth Army Corps.

In June 1982, Saddam ordered a unilateral pullback to the border and appealed to Iran to stop fighting so that both countries could join forces against Israel, which had just invaded Lebanon. Khomeini was unmoved.

Iraqi honor guards march to Martyrs' Monument in Baghdad marking the anniversary of the end of the Iran–Iraq war, August 8, 1999. REUTERS

Iran launched repeated offensives in the next couple of years, making some territorial gains at an appalling cost in human life, but failing to capture the main prize of Basra. It scored a notable success in capturing the Majnoon Islands in the Hawizeh marshland of southern Iraq in March 1984. Iraq meanwhile concentrated on a desperate defense of its own territory.

His back to the wall, Saddam took bold steps to counter the mortal threat to Iraq and his own position. As a war of attrition ground on from 1984 to 1987, he survived with help from many outside powers, especially the United States, France, the Soviet Union and pro-Western Arab states, which could not contemplate an Iraqi defeat by Khomeini's Iran. He used chemical weapons to blunt Iranian offensives and counter the enemy's advantage in manpower. He fired missiles at Iranian population centers in early 1984, triggering a "War of the Cities" that cost thousands of civilian lives on each side, but failed to dent Iranian morale. And he tried to incite superpower intervention to end the war by attacking Iranian shipping in the Gulf.

From the start of the war, Saddam had won generous financial backing from Saudi Arabia, Kuwait and other Gulf states, which lent him anywhere up to $50 billion.

Irangate Jolts Region

Iran, generally at a disadvantage in arms procurement, had to turn to such unlikely suppliers as Israel and Vietnam in its scramble for spares for its U.S.-made arsenal inherited from the Shah. It also bought arms from North Korea and China. In 1985, however, U.S. President Ronald Reagan's administration struck a secret deal with Iran, selling it antitank missiles in exchange for the release of American hostages kidnapped in Lebanon. Further deals in which U.S. weapons were channeled to Iran through Israel, with the Reagan administration sending the proceeds covertly to U.S.-backed Contra guerrillas in Nicaragua, took place in 1986. But in November, a Lebanese magazine revealed the arms-for-hostages trafficking and gave details of a bizarre, secret visit to Tehran that former U.S. National Security Adviser Robert McFarlane had undertaken in May in a futile bid to improve U.S.–Iranian relations.

The ensuing scandal astonished the world, rocked the Reagan presidency and left the flavor of betrayal in Baghdad and the capitals of Washington's Arab allies. They could scarcely believe that the United States could arm Iran, its bitter foe, or so blatantly violate its own declared policy of refusing to negotiate with terrorists.

The United States, while not wanting to see Iraq comprehensively defeated, showed little interest in halting a war that was conveniently sapping the energies of two sworn enemies of Israel, its closest regional ally. Yet the Irangate scandal prompted the United States to tighten an arms blockade against Iran and to reassure its Gulf Arab allies with increased military assistance. It stepped up economic aid, particularly agricultural credit, and military intelligence to Iraq.

Despite Irangate, Iraq held an overall edge in keeping up the flow of arms from abroad. The Soviet Union, Iraq's traditional supplier, initially signaled its disapproval of the war by imposing an arms embargo on both sides, but resumed shipments to Iraq in 1982. The West, apart from France, had banned sales of "lethal weapons" to both sides, a formula that almost invited circumvention. In 1983, France supplied Iraq with Mirage F-1 fighter-bombers and leased it Super-Etendard aircraft for use with Exocet antiship missiles. Saudi Arabia shipped weapons to Iraq and shared military intelligence from U.S. satellite pictures and American-manned AWACS surveillance planes leased to Riyadh from 1981.

In August 1982, Saddam signaled his intention to throttle Iran's main surviving oil export outlet by declaring a maritime exclusion zone around the Kharg Island terminal in the Gulf. This drew a warning from Khomeini that if Iran's oil exports were hit, "not a drop of oil" would flow through the Strait of Hormuz, the conduit for one-sixth of Western oil needs. That threat brought extra U.S., British and French naval forces to the Gulf.

Tanker War Breaks Out

Iraq intensified the "Tanker War" in 1984, using its air superiority to attack Iran's ports and tankers in the Gulf. It began using the Exocet-armed Super-Etendards to hit tankers in March and struck at Kharg in May. Since no Iraqi oil was exported from the Gulf, Iran retaliated by attacking ships trading with Iraq's allies, Saudi Arabia and Kuwait, without taking responsibility. Damage to the Kharg terminal in December 1984 prompted Iran to start shuttling oil from Kharg to Sirri Island lower in the Gulf. Iraqi planes launched sustained strikes on Kharg in August 1985. The following year Iraq launched long-range air raids on oil facilities at Sirri Island and Larak.

The U.S. military said that by January 1987 the Iraqis had carried out 132 attacks on Gulf shipping to Iran's 70 since the start of the Tanker War. Iran, which had installed Silkworm antiship missiles at the mouth of the Gulf, threatened in March to halt oil shipments through the Strait of Hormuz. The Soviet Union then allowed Kuwait to claim its protection by chartering three Soviet tankers. Ironically it was an

American sailors on the *USS Stark* off the coast of Bahrain, May 19, 1987. An Iraqi plane two days earlier hit the vessel with a missile, killing 37 American sailors and leaving the gaping hole. REUTERS

Iraqi missile attack on the U.S. frigate *Stark* on May 17, 1987, in which 37 American crewmen were killed, which sealed U.S. involvement. Washington accepted Iraq's apology for the error.

The Reagan administration then reregistered 11 Kuwaiti tankers under the U.S. flag and sent the biggest naval armada assembled since the Vietnam War to the Gulf to defend "freedom of navigation" against Iranian threats. Several European nations sent minesweepers. The U.S. Navy began escorting Kuwaiti tankers flying the Stars and Stripes in July and soon used its firepower. In one devastating action in April 1988, U.S. warships blew up two Iranian oil rigs and destroyed several Iranian naval vessels. Three months later, the U.S. cruiser *Vincennes* shot down an Iran Air airbus killing all 290 people on board, after mistaking it for an F-14 warplane.

To stave off defeat, Iraq repeatedly used chemical weapons from its home-produced stocks of mustard gas and nerve agents. Its technicians learned how to load these into rockets, artillery shells, aerial bombs and warheads on the al-Hussein Scud missile variant. Iraq

Distraught Iranians gather at Dubai airport awaiting news of relatives aboard an Iranian airliner shot down by a U.S. missile from the *USS Vincennes*, July 3, 1988. The *Vincennes* wrongly identified the airliner as a warplane. All 290 passengers and crew were killed. REUTERS

used mustard gas as early as 1983 in the northern sector of the front. In March 1984, Major General Maher Abdul-Rashid, commander of Iraq's Third Corps, said he would welcome the chance to use "an insecticide to wipe out the bothersome swarms of insects."

United Nations investigators repeatedly accused Iraq of using chemical weapons in violation of the 1925 Geneva Protocol, but the international outcry was muted. Even Iraq's use of poison gas against its own Kurds in April 1987 brought only verbal condemnation. But the chemical bombing that killed around 5,000 residents of Halabja on March 16, 1988, shortly after its capture by Iranian forces and Iraqi Kurdish rebels, had a profound impact on Iran. Iranian leaders worried that Baghdad might fire chemical warheads into their cities if its forces were being overrun.

Iraq used its chemical arsenal extensively in the recapture of the Faw peninsula and Shalamcheh in April and May 1988, and the following month in the seizure of the Iranian town of Mehran and the retaking of the Majnoon Islands. This sapped Iranian morale. Chemical attacks affected some 100,000 Iranians, including about 10,000 who died quickly. Up to 5,000 are reported to remain under medical surveillance, many with damaged lungs. "Our neighbors' son was sent to Sweden to be treated for internal chemical burns," a young Tehran woman told me. "It failed and he came home. He never worked or did anything, just sat outside the house until he died. I could not bear to look at him."

By the final year of the war, Iran knew that most of the world was ranged against it. United States readiness to challenge Iran militarily in the Gulf had bolstered Iraq, as had military supplies flowing in from

Iran–Iraq War Chronology

1980

Sep 7 Iraq accuses Iran of shelling Iraqi border towns from territory belonging to Iraq under 1975 Algiers agreement on frontier line and Shatt al-Arab waterway. Ten days later President Saddam Hussein tears up Algiers accord.

Sep 22 Iraqi troops invade Iran.

Sep 28 Saddam says that the invasion was a pre-emptive strike in the face of imminent Iranian attack. Iraq captures the Iranian port of Khorramshahr.

1981

Jun 7 Israeli planes attack and destroy the Osirak nuclear reactor near Baghdad.

1982

Mar Iran launches ground offensive and retakes Khorramshahr.

1983

Iran threatens to seal off Strait of Hormuz—then a lifeline for world oil supplies—if Iraq takes delivery of new weapons from France.

1984

Mar Iranian Revolutionary Guards thrust across on the southern front and capture Iraq's oil-rich Majnoon Islands.

Apr Iraq attacks Gulf oil tankers using the loading terminal at Kharg Island to reduce Iranian oil exports.

Nov 26 Iraq and the United States establish full diplomatic relations, which were terminated in 1967 after U.S. support for Israel.

1986

Feb Iran captures the Iraqi port of Faw in an offensive.

Nov 13 U.S. President Reagan admits secret arms sales to Iran. Twelve days later it is disclosed that funds from these arms sales had been diverted to aid the U.S.-backed Contras battling Nicaragua's leftist Sandinista government.

1987

Jan 8 Iran launches major offensive toward Basra, viewed as one of the war's major actions. United States officials say that about 45,000 Iranian and 25,000 Iraqi troops are killed around Basra in a five-week period.

May 17 Iraq attacks the *USS Stark* protecting Gulf shipping—37 aboard are killed. Saddam apologizes, saying it was an error.

1988

Jan United Nations says more than 167 ships were attacked in the Gulf in 1987, over 50 percent more than the previous year.

Feb 29 Tehran comes under long-range missile attack for the first time. Thousands of civilians are killed on both sides in "war of the cities."

Mar Iran seizes the town of Halabja in northeastern Iraq. Tehran says that Iraq used chemical weapons to punish inhabitants for not resisting. It says 5,000 were killed.

Apr Elite Iraqi forces recapture the port of Faw. In June they also take back the Majnoon Islands, retaking all the territory lost to Iran since 1984.

Jul 3 U.S. warship *Vincennes* shoots down an Iran Air A-300 Airbus in the Strait of Hormuz after wrongly identifying it as an attacking fighter. All 290 people on board are killed.

(continued)

Jul 18   Iran says it accepts Security Council resolution 598 adopted in July 1987 as a formula for ending the war.

Aug 6   Iraq and Iran agree to begin peace negotiations.

Aug 20   Ceasefire officially implemented and monitored by U.N. Iran–Iraq Military Observer Group (UNIIMOG).

the Soviet Union. For the first time in six years, Iran lacked the volunteers and the organization to launch a major winter offensive. Iraq scored lightning victories, recovered much of its lost territory and mounted fresh offensives even after Tehran's unconditional acceptance of the U.N. ceasefire resolution in July.

Massive Loss of Life

Both sides had suffered enormous losses while fighting each other to a standstill in a conflict that failed to resolve the original issues. After the collapse of his dreams of a military triumph, Saddam announced in 1985 that defending Iraq until the other side stopped attacking would constitute victory. Iranian leaders, some of whom had vowed to replace Saddam's "atheist" rule with an Islamic state, failed to achieve even their minimal objectives of toppling the Iraqi leader, getting an international inquiry to blame Iraq for the war and receiving reparations. The war ended with secular Baathists still in power in Iraq and Islamic revolutionaries still ruling Iran.

To shore up national unity, Saddam had sought the legitimacy of Islam, casting the struggle in a religious as well as a nationalist context. Determined to pursue a guns-and-butter policy regardless of the war, he burdened his country with crippling debts. Iraq is estimated to have spent $95 billion on the war, in addition to foreign loans and grants totaling $85–90 billion. Iran by contrast spent only $85 billion and refused to borrow abroad. Nevertheless, the war effectively contained any ambition Tehran might have had to export its revolution by force of arms—to the relief of both the superpowers of the day and its regional neighbors.

By the time the guns fell silent, Iraq had a tenth of its population under arms—a standing army of one million and a 600,000-strong armed militia. Iran, with a population of about 50 million, could only match the Iraqi figure. But Iraq's military superiority over Iran at the end of the war was to prove short-lived, thanks to the mauling its forces suffered in the 1991 Gulf War.

Iraq's annexation of Kuwait in August 1990 produced the first real breakthrough in peace negotiations that had bogged down after the 1988 ceasefire. Saddam, seeking to secure his eastern flank, accepted key Iranian demands, including the restoration of the Algiers Accord and withdrawals from border areas still occupied by Iraq. Prisoner exchanges began, and diplomatic relations were restored in September. The United Nations verified on February 20, 1991, that the two sides had withdrawn all their forces to the internationally recognized border.

Unfinished Business: The Legacy of U.S. Intervention in the Gulf

David Storey

"We need the humility to recognize that, while America has capabilities, we are not invulnerable—and our current situation is not a permanent condition. If we don't act now, new threats will emerge to surprise us, as they have so often in the past."

U.S. Defense Secretary Donald Rumsfeld
in testimony to Congress,
June 21, 2001

Oil, the thick black blood that ran through the veins of world industry and human activity throughout the 20th century, inspired and shaped U.S. interests in Iraq. Securing that lifeblood against rivals—including opposing powers in two world wars and the Soviet Union—focused the attention of planners in Washington on a distant and very foreign place which might otherwise have been chiefly of interest to American students as a cradle of ancient civilization, the home of the Hanging Gardens of Babylon, the eastern frontier of the Arab world.

But by the start of the 21st century, a different and even greater interest became paramount—U.S.

national security. Oil had attracted and held America's attention, but the measures Washington took to maintain control of supplies, sometimes riding roughshod over local sensitivities, bred fierce anti-American feelings. After spectacular attacks against a string of U.S. targets by disaffected Muslims bent on driving America out of the region, the September 11 attacks on the United States itself finally prompted a major shift in the U.S. approach. Where threats had been contained, now they had broken out. Where previously there had been uncomfortable pinpricks against the superpower, now America itself was shown to be open to massive attack against which its traditional defenses were useless.

During 2002, as President George W. Bush prepared his country for war against Iraq, the issue of oil was scarcely mentioned. Many experts believe the structure of world supplies now means there would be no major oil shock following a new Iraq war—a spike in prices, to be sure, but nothing the world market could not handle. There would probably be a medium-term price fall as more Iraqi oil came to the market, they said. The main concern was not that Iraq would turn off the taps, halting production of some 1.7 million barrels of oil a day, but that it would continue to use revenues from sales of that oil to build chemical, biological or nuclear weapons that it could use either to blackmail the West or hand to extremist groups to use directly against America.

But whatever the focus of U.S. concern today, it is important to understand that the crisis the United States now faces is in large part the legacy of a century of oil-driven engagement.

The Oil Rush

After the failure of several explorations in the Gulf area at the turn of the last century, British capitalist William Knox D'Arcy, who had made a fortune from gold mining in Australia, finally struck oil at Masjed Soleyman in Iran in May 1908. The first oil field discovered in Iraq was near Kirkuk in the north in 1927.

With the United States leading the way, the demand for petroleum, particularly to drive cars and trucks, had accelerated. Henry Ford was rolling his popular automobile models off the production lines. In World War One motor vehicles began to replace horses, and the world did not look back, in war or peacetime. After World War Two, the British Empire, the big South Asian power, was in rapid decline and the Soviet Union was trying to expand its reach to the south. Washington accepted the importance of securing the Gulf region's oil for itself and its allies.

With Britain struggling to maintain its waning influence in an independent Iraq, the United States committed military force to the area, stationing a small naval task force at the northern Gulf island of Bahrain. That presence became firmly planted. Bahrain's capital, Manama, now houses the headquarters of the U.S. Fifth Fleet.

U.S. AND BRITISH FORCES IN STRIKING RANGE OF IRAQ

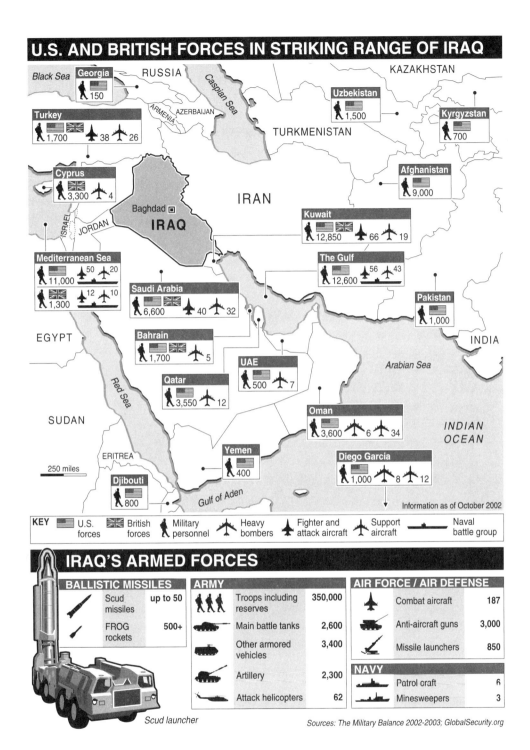

Black Sea

Georgia 150

RUSSIA

KAZAKHSTAN

Turkey 1,700 — 38 — 26

ARMENIA AZERBAIJAN Caspian Sea

Uzbekistan 1,500

Kyrgyzstan 700

TURKMENISTAN

Cyprus 3,300 — 4

Baghdad ▣
IRAQ

IRAN

Afghanistan 9,000

ISRAEL JORDAN

Kuwait 12,850 — 66 — 19

Mediterranean Sea 11,000 — 50 — 20 / 1,300 — 12 — 10

The Gulf 12,600 — 56 — 43

Saudi Arabia 6,600 — 40 — 32

Pakistan 1,000

EGYPT

Bahrain 1,700 — 5

INDIA

UAE 500 — 7

Arabian Sea

Qatar 3,550 — 12

Red Sea

SUDAN

Oman 3,600 — 6 — 34

INDIAN OCEAN

ERITREA

250 miles

Yemen 400

Diego Garcia 1,000 — 8 — 12

Djibouti 800

Gulf of Aden

Information as of October 2002

KEY U.S. forces | British forces | Military personnel | Heavy bombers | Fighter and attack aircraft | Support aircraft | Naval battle group

---

IRAQ'S ARMED FORCES

BALLISTIC MISSILES

Scud missiles	up to 50
FROG rockets	500+

ARMY

Troops including reserves	350,000
Main battle tanks	2,600
Other armored vehicles	3,400
Artillery	2,300
Attack helicopters	62

AIR FORCE / AIR DEFENSE

Combat aircraft	187
Anti-aircraft guns	3,000
Missile launchers	850

NAVY

Patrol craft	6
Minesweepers	3

Scud launcher

Sources: The Military Balance 2002-2003; GlobalSecurity.org

President George W. Bush (right) talks to his father, former President George Bush, and former Secretary of State James Baker (center) as they watch the inaugural parade outside the White House in Washington, January 20, 2001. George W. Bush took the oath of office as 43rd president of the United States. REUTERS

The United States has always played an open and a clandestine game in the region. It worked, sometimes with Britain, to put down revolts, install and massage friendly governments and ensure that the oil kept flowing and that the Russians were kept in check. In 1953 the CIA helped install the Shah of Iran in Tehran.

The United States was already committed to a rash of conflicts against the Soviet Union around the world, notably in Vietnam, and its strategy for the critical oil source in the Gulf was to build up two regional powers—Iran and Saudi Arabia—providing them with enormous arsenals and economic advantages to ensure their loyalty to the West and the stability of their autocratic rulers. Washington hoped to prevent either of these Islamic states from becoming too powerful in its own right. At the same time, it channeled the two countries away from an aggressive stand toward Israel, as the United States emerged as the embattled Jewish state's main protector.

Proxy Strategy Fails

That strategy fell apart in January 1979, when the Shah of Iran was forced out by Ayatollah Ruhollah Khomeini's Islamic revolution, a cataclysmic upheaval that cast doubts on the United States' grip on the undercurrents of world politics, particularly in the Muslim world.

By the 1970s, American, British and other interests in most Gulf oil-producing states had long been nationalized, but there was still a deep antagonism and mistrust of the United States as it tried to manipulate events to its advantage.

In Iraq, Saddam Hussein had gradually been amassing power as the cold-blooded enforcer under the leadership of Ahmed Hassan al-Bakr. American involvement with Saddam began soon after he took over the presidency himself in July 1979, at the age of 42. He drew in all the strings of military and civil power and eliminated any possible rivals in a series of ferocious Stalinist purges.

Washington knew Saddam's record, but the actions of Khomeini in his eastern neighbor Iran were even more threatening. The Iranian revolution, which jeopardized stability in the entire Gulf region, became personal for America when the U.S. embassy was seized by revolutionary students on November 4, 1979, and 52 hostages were held for 444 days.

So Americans quietly cheered, and helped, when Saddam invaded Iran in 1980. The United States was not blind to his abuses, which by then had included cruelty against opponents and their families. They were aware of his close links with Communist Russia. They knew of his long-standing commitment to drive the Israelis into the Mediterranean Sea. But Iran had become the bigger challenge. Khomeini was the greater of two evils.

Saddam as "Friend"

Shortly after the Iran–Iraq war started, the U.S. administration led by President Ronald Reagan removed Iraq from its list of terrorist-sponsoring nations and then stood by mutely as Saddam used chemical weapons both on Iranian forces and on his own Kurdish minority. This was an irony in 2002 when Washington prepared to go to war against Iraq, specifically citing its links with international terrorism and its development of weapons of mass destruction. During the Iran–Iraq war Washington gave Saddam intelligence from U.S. satellites about the position of Iranian forces and provided him with helicopters.

The U.S.–Iraqi relationship was based entirely on expediency. Thus it did not appear to falter when it was revealed in 1986 that President Reagan had also been selling arms to Iran in what became known as the Iran–Contra scandal—a secret attempt to secure the release of Americans held hostage in Lebanon by the Iran-backed Hizbollah group. Some of the arms were delivered through Israel. This two-timing would surely have upset Saddam, but he cannot have been shocked. His dealings with America had never been based on trust, on either side. Indeed, many U.S. analysts believed it was in Washington's

Secretary of Defense Donald Rumsfeld (right) listens to Army General Tommy Franks, head of U.S. Central Command, while answering questions during a Pentagon briefing about the campaign that ousted Afghanistan's Taliban government, November 15, 2001. REUTERS

interest to prolong the war, to see that no dominant power was established in the region.

When he came to office in 1989, President George H. W. Bush inherited a policy of treating Saddam gingerly, but as a leader who could be dealt with, despite his obvious drawbacks. Kenneth Pollack, who was the Gulf expert in President Bill Clinton's national security council in the 1990s, wrote in his 2002 book *The Threatening Storm,* "Washington had worked so hard to ignore Saddam's obvious flaws that it had essentially convinced itself that Saddam was little different from other brutal dictators with whom the United States had developed long and profitable relationships."

Saddam as Enemy

Bush was quickly disabused of any such notion in August 1990 when Saddam, heading a huge army hardened by years of war, in a financial crunch and feeling he had the Arab world behind him, began his second big adventure. He invaded Kuwait. For the United States, he was now unquestionably and irrevocably an enemy, a pariah outside the game.

After leading an international coalition to drive Iraqi forces out of Kuwait in 1991, the United States adopted a policy of containment with occasional flashes of fierce reprisal. This included a barrage of cruise missiles on Baghdad in 1993 after a foiled attempt to assassinate the former President Bush when he visited Kuwait in April that year. Some saw in that incident the seeds of George W. Bush's commitment to overthrow Saddam, although much more is at play for the President than a simple desire to avenge a plot against his father.

In 1998, when United Nations weapons inspectors finally left the country after being frustrated in their search for biological, chemical and nuclear weapons under a post-Gulf War mandate, the United States and Britain unleashed Operation Desert Fox, flying more than 600 aircraft sorties and launching more than 400 cruise missiles, saying the aim was to "degrade" weapons-of-mass-destruction programs which inspections had failed to halt.

One incident in the 1990s—a failed attempt in 1995 to spark a rebellion—has had repercussions for later approaches to ousting Saddam. Fed with information by the defecting head of the Iraqi intelligence service, Wafiq al-Samarra'i, and accompanied by CIA field agents and a handful of members of the opposition Iraqi National Congress (INC), some Kurdish forces staged an attack on a dispirited Iraqi military unit near Arbil. They were hoping to dislodge the first stone that would create an avalanche, draw in U.S. military support and drive Saddam from power. They miscalculated. Saddam sent loyal and powerful forces to crush the advance. United States backing never came.

The incident has not been forgotten in Washington. It colored every consideration of fomenting internal uprising to unseat Saddam and undermined hopes that the INC, a loose alliance of squabbling and disparate groups, could act as an agent of change, although it might have a role once change was in motion.

In the meantime the "containment" approach continued. It depended on United Nations sanctions, which had become increasingly ineffective over the years, and enforcement of "no-fly" zones over northern and southern areas. The United States essentially ran a holding operation in the 1990s under President Clinton, who was taken up with the aftermath of the end of the Cold War, Middle East peace moves, war in the Balkans, roller-coaster relations with an emerging China and more domestic issues.

A U.S. Marine looks through the sights of an antitank gun at the start of the three-week "Eager Mace 2000" exercise in the Kuwaiti desert, April 1, 2000. REUTERS

Agitation for Action

There was always a potent faction in Washington urging tougher action against Baghdad. Many senior U.S. officials, particularly Republicans who worked under the first President Bush, had been deeply disturbed by the indecisive end of the Gulf War and Saddam's resumption of weapons programs. Their frustration boiled to the surface in an open letter to Clinton in early 1998, in which a group of former foreign and security policymakers urged him to act militarily to stop Iraq's development of nuclear, biological and chemical weapons and to work through "diplomatic, political and military efforts" to remove Saddam from power. The letter said: "The security of the world in the first part of the 21st century will be determined largely by how we handle this threat."

Later that year Clinton signed the Iraq Liberation Act, which enshrined "regime change" in Baghdad as American policy, but there was no sign he was prepared to take decisive action against Saddam, who was opposed by Russia as well as many European states and the Arab world.

Four years later, with George W. Bush in the White House and Americans still assessing their vulnerability after the attacks of September 11, 2001, much of the rhetoric about Iraq echoed the language of the 1998 open letter. This was not surprising. Many of those who had signed the letter were by then running Bush's policy. They included Defense Secretary Donald Rumsfeld, Deputy Defense Secretary Paul Wolfowitz, Undersecretary of State John Bolton and Zalmay Khalilzad, who as the top official on the region on Bush's national security council wielded immense influence. A decade after overseeing a policy that failed to settle the Saddam threat under the first President Bush, the same people were back in power, and this time they were determined to fix the problem.

It's a New World

Many things in the world were different, but the biggest changes were the nature of the threat to American security and the lifting of some restraints on U.S. action.

Rumsfeld, an old fox of a politician who has been involved with Washington's defense planning on and off for three decades, argued from the start of the new Bush government that the national security mold based for half a century on the Moscow–Washington rivalry must be replaced, not just adapted. Russia was now America's friend. The threat of mutual annihilation was no longer what bound the peace.

Precisely what the new threat was, Rumsfeld could not say, as he argued in the administration's first few months for a complete and costly overhaul of the American military, which had been cut back after the collapse of the Soviet Union. But, he argued, many major upheavals, like the end of Soviet Communism itself or the invasion of Kuwait by Saddam in 1990, had not been on the radar screens of planners before they occurred.

"We need the humility to recognize that, while America has capabilities, we are not invulnerable—and our current situation is not a permanent condition. If we don't act now, new threats will emerge to surprise us, as they have so often in the past," he said in testimony to Congress on June 21, 2001. This was prophetic. Less than three months later came the attacks on the World Trade Center and the Pentagon, which destroyed Americans' sense of security and plunged the country into a new war—the War on Terrorism.

The immediate target of that new war was the al Qaeda Islamic movement of Osama bin Laden, accused of carrying out the attacks. No strong links have been drawn between al Qaeda and Saddam. But Iraq quickly fit into the picture of the broader threat. Bush said it formed an "axis of evil" with Iran and North Korea—states that were developing weapons of mass destruction and at the same time backing international terrorism. In Bush's words, the gravest danger to the United States "lies at the crossroads of radicalism and technology." Saddam's Iraq lay at that crossroads.

A U.S. soldier covers up his face against a sandstorm at his compound in the Kuwaiti desert, September 17, 1996. REUTERS

Danger of Sneak Attacks

The danger to America came now from sneak attacks by nonstate groups undeterred by threats of reprisal, driven not by economic or strategic motives but by less definable and more scattered objectives. Bush argued that Saddam, who had sprung wars on his neighbors Iran and Kuwait and had lied about everything from his capabilities to his intentions, was hurrying to build a nuclear weapon that he could either use himself or put in the hands of such international terrorists, changing the world balance of power.

This was the new threat, perhaps the only threat that could seriously challenge the supreme and only superpower, whose global military might and economic clout dwarfed that of all other states or alliances.

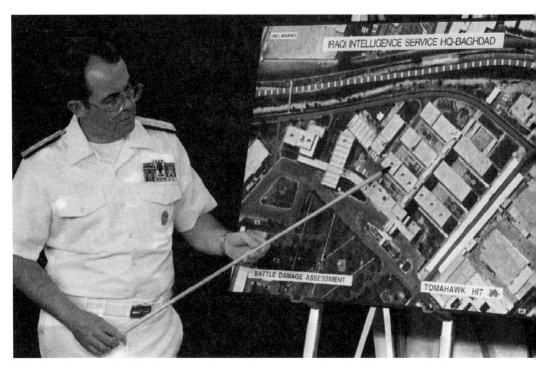

U.S. Navy Rear Admiral Mike Cramer points out Tomahawk cruise missile hits on an Iraqi intelligence compound during a Pentagon briefing, June 27, 1993. The strikes were ordered after an attempted assassination of former President Bush on a visit to Kuwait on April 15, 1993. REUTERS

The new challenge prompted a shift in strategy and a transformation in Bush, the former Texas governor whose knowledge of the world beyond America's borders was rudimentary at best before he ran for office. He had told electoral campaign meetings then that Washington must project its power "humbly." He was dismissive of what he called "nation building" by the Clinton administration, a reference to efforts to create some order in chaotic states like Somalia and rebuild civil institutions in the Balkans. There were too many U.S. forces stationed around the world, Bush declared, meddling in conflicts that the United States need not be a part of.

But the shock of the September 11 attacks and a growing awareness of the vulnerability of the open U.S. society transformed his lack of interest in foreign policy into evangelical zeal. Washington had to confront its enemies on their own turf, take the fight to the enemy. Other countries were expected to fall in line with Washington's world view. In Bush's words, "You are either with us or against us."

Most countries were indeed with Washington in the battle against the tentacles of al Qaeda and the blitzkrieg that smashed its home base, Taliban-ruled Afghanistan, in the winter of 2001–2. That was not a difficult call. Very many countries, developed and developing, had suffered from terror attacks.

Doctrine of Pre-emption

But the new "forward leaning" U.S. stand, especially over the urgent need to oust Saddam and destroy his weapons programs, went further. The principles were set out formally in a new National Security Strategy issued by Bush in September 2002. It said America should use its "unparalleled military strength and great economic and political influence" to establish a balance of power that "favors human freedom" and is aimed at defeating the threat from "terrorists and tyrants." The document said that in the future the United States would allow no one to remotely challenge its power and America would "not hesitate to act alone, if necessary, to exercise our right of self-defense by acting pre-emptively."

Anti-war protesters pass Big Ben and the Houses of Parliament during a rally in London, September 28, 2002. REUTERS

In essence this meant attacking before a threat materialized. A classic precedent cited by some U.S. officials was the destruction by Israel of the Egyptian air force as Egypt was poised to invade Israel in the 1967 war. Rumsfeld has used another example—the blockade of Cuba in 1962 to stop Russia from using the island as a launch pad for nuclear missiles aimed at the United States. Perhaps the most appropriate precedent was Israel's bombing of Iraq's Osirak nuclear facility in 1981, which halted, or at least set back, the very threat that

Washington confronted 20 years later. It is an interesting measure of the radical change in American thinking that the Israeli raid drew stiff U.S. criticism at the time, with America joining in a United Nations resolution condemning it.

And so to "Regime Change"

Against this background the Bush administration decided that war against Iraq was essential to neutralize Saddam unless he took the very unlikely step of allowing unfettered access for U.N. weapons inspectors and destruction of any illegal arms programs they found. He also had to fulfill a list of other intrusive demands made in U.N. resolutions since Saddam's 1990 invasion of Kuwait. To suggest that he might actually comply was described by White House spokesman Ari Fleischer as "the mother of all hypotheticals"—a mocking reference to Saddam's threatening the United States with "the mother of all battles" before the lopsided 1991 Gulf War.

Throughout 2002, urged on by hardliners in his administration including Rumsfeld, Wolfowitz and Vice President Dick Cheney, President Bush beat the drums of war, making clear Saddam was an evil and looming danger who must be removed. But they grew coy when asked exactly how this would be done. Largely because of counsel from Secretary of State Colin Powell, the administration accepted that, with almost the entire world opposing a U.S. assault, it was necessary to attract international backing through the United Nations. This was not so much to help with the military operation—although use of facilities in Turkey and the Gulf states was essential for the scale of operation needed—but to ensure that the international community would cooperate with the United States in Iraq after a war.

How to Oust Saddam?

Various U.S. options for ousting Saddam were discussed in the diplomatic and political warm-up to action through 2002. Memories of the failed 1995 plot and the knowledge that Saddam's army, still one of the world's biggest, possessed considerable power, including large stocks of biological and chemical weapons, cast early doubts on one widely touted strategy, the so-called "Afghan model." The rapid victory over the Taliban had relied on heavy U.S. air bombardments and backing for the opposition Northern Alliance, which swept the Taliban from Kabul.

In Iraq, this approach was originally advocated by the leaders of the Iraqi National Congress, the squabbling group of opposition forces including the two big Kurdish factions (the Kurdistan Democratic Party and the Patriotic Union of Kurdistan), an Iranian-backed Shi'ite movement and several smaller exile groups. Such an approach could be based either on using some 50,000 armed forces from the two main Kurdish groups, which have been unwilling to get involved without solid American commitments, or on carving out a haven in southern or western Iraq, from which an opposition group, with U.S. air support, might advance on Baghdad.

Many experts were skeptical about relying on such risky allies for a historic undertaking of this sort. General Anthony Zinni, the former head of Central Command, which oversees U.S. forces in the region, said this could lead to a "Bay of Goats," a pointed reference to the disastrous 1961 "Bay of Pigs" operation launched by Cuban exiles against Communist President Fidel Castro.

Late in 2002, the United States approved spending $92 million to give military training to about 5,000 opposition members under the Iraqi National Congress. But they would be battlefield advisers, scouts and interpreters with U.S. forces, not actually fighting Saddam's troops. The more opposition forces are involved, the more likely it is Saddam will infiltrate them, as he has done successfully in the past.

Most U.S. experts discount the "Afghan model," as well as any attempt to foment a coup within Iraq or arrange for the Iraqi leader's assassination unless this were part of a broader plan involving a major U.S. military campaign. Such proposals entailed too much uncertainty, they believe, although the White House's Fleischer let slip a crude reference to such an idea as late as October 2002. Asked at a briefing about congressional cost estimates of $9 billion to $13 billion for a start up to an Iraq war, Fleischer said: "The cost of one bullet the Iraqi people take on themselves is substantially less than that."

Full Frontal Assault

Various plans for a possible war found their way into the media during the year, but it was not clear whether they were deliberately put out as red herrings to distract the Iraqis, or perhaps by discontented officers hoping to sway the debate. In mid-November officials said Bush had approved the outline of a plan that involved swiftly capturing footholds in the country to act as springboards for a force that would eventually grow to 200,000 to 250,000 troops. The operation would begin with an air campaign in which B-1 and B-2 bombers aimed at cutting off Saddam's power base, attacking his air defenses, palaces and military with 1,000-pound satellite-guided bombs. Unmanned spy planes, some armed with missiles and Special Operations forces would play an important early role as the United States sought out chemical and biological weapons and Saddam's small number of medium-range Scud missiles. One official said U.S. planners hoped for the collapse of Saddam's administration within weeks. "We've made it clear ... that there is little profit for his military to stand up and fight," he said.

While Washington would need to enlist help from friendly neighboring states and some countries, notably Britain, would almost certainly be integrated into the attack, the plan would not rely on fickle partners and would bring the quickest possible and most certain military victory. Pollack, Clinton's former regional adviser, said it was the surest, most sensible approach. "If we decide to topple (Saddam) overtly, we need to hit him as hard as we can and move as fast as we can to take down his regime before he can inflict significant damage," he said in *The Threatening Storm*. That damage could come in the form of chemical or biological attacks on U.S. forces or on its allies.

In October, Israeli Prime Minister Ariel Sharon received a promise from Bush when he visited Washington that U.S. forces would work to protect Israel in the event of war. The United States was determined to try to keep Israel from being drawn into such a conflict for fear of igniting a wider Middle East war. Saddam, one of the most vitriolic anti-Israeli Arab leaders, is deeply hated in Israel. He has been paying money to the families of Palestinians who blow themselves up as suicide bombers in the hostilities inside Israel.

The Pentagon quietly began in 2002 to move shiploads of heavy equipment to the region, adding to big stockpiles of armor, missiles and ammunition the United States has kept in the Gulf since the 1991

A man with a cut-out face of President George W. Bush attached to his back joins thousands of anti-war demonstrators in New York's Central Park protesting a possible U.S. military strike on Iraq, October 6, 2002. REUTERS

war. In other signs of war readiness, two aircraft battle groups were ordered to the Gulf area late in the year, ostensibly to replace two carriers already in place, but all four could stay on station if needed. In addition military analysts said two other carrier battle groups—one based in San Diego and the other in Yokosuka, Japan—could be brought into the area quickly.

Various command units were moved to the Gulf for exercises, and the Pentagon left open the possibility of how long they might stay. They included an army corps headquarters from Germany. More significantly, 600 members of the U.S. Central Command based in Tampa, Florida, headed by the man who would oversee any war against

From the Streets of the Iraqi Capital

Samia Nakhoul

First there was the Iran–Iraq war, then there was the Gulf War. Iraq survived both of them, and today, as the country faces the prospect of a third war, the mood is one of fatalism.

"We have a saying in Iraq: 'Those who are already wet aren't scared of rain.' What is there to be afraid of?" says Ahmed Falah, an engineer.

"We believe that what has been written by God for us will happen. Nobody likes war, but if someone comes and invades your country, what would you do? Wouldn't you fight?" asks businessman Wahab Ahmad.

Iraqis, once a cultured and traveled people, feel isolated as never before after 12 years of U.N. sanctions that have wrecked their economy and cut them off from the world. But despite the privations that sanctions have brought, they try to live as normal lives as possible. Coffee shops are packed with men smoking water pipes and playing backgammon. Weddings are celebrated in traditional style. Some people are even building new homes.

Teenagers hang out in Baghdad's new computer centers, most of them hooked on computer war games in which the enemy is invariably the United States.

"This is between us and our enemy," says Ihab Bashar, 14, as he and his friends play the latest shoot-'em-up video game. "It is like us versus America and Britain."

Fingers clicking on the console, Ihab shoots at helicopters with a multibarrel rocket launcher. The helicopters explode with satisfying regularity. Soldiers parachute out. He turns his fire on the soldiers, and the war goes on.

In Baghdad, the most obvious damage from the Gulf War in 1991 has been erased. Bridges, roads and government buildings destroyed by allied bombings during the war and by U.S.–British air strikes in 1998 have been rebuilt. Streets are bustling with cars and shoppers. Even old public buses have been replaced with new ones. The streets are brightly lit at night, and palm trees line the large and newly asphalted highways. The city appears to be functioning. Yet its people look exhausted from years of isolation and deprivation.

There is virtually no sign of hoarding or stockpiling of goods. Not many people can afford it anyway. "Stock up on what? And with what money?" lamented one Baghdad resident. The government has, however, begun supplying Iraqis with food rations for two months in advance under the U.N. oil-for-food program, introduced in 1996 to ease the burden on ordinary Iraqis.

According to U.N. statistics, there is more medicine available and more food in people's stomachs thanks to that program, which allows Baghdad to sell some

A four-year-old Iraqi boy suffering from cancer is comforted by his mother in a children's hospital in Baghdad, January 27, 2001. Baghdad insisted that there was a link between depleted uranium shells fired by allied forces and a rise in the number of Iraqis suffering from leukemia and other cancers. Western health officials steadfastly contest this assertion. REUTERS

(continued)

oil and import civilian necessities with the proceeds. But try telling parents at the Mansour Hospital for Children, where youngsters with cancer lie dying from what Iraqi doctors say are the effects of the Gulf War, that things are getting better.

"Look! These are the children of Iraq," said Nouhad Abdel-Amir, pointing at the cancer ward packed with frail children with no hair, many lying unconscious with drips strapped to their bodies. She herself was holding her one-year-old baby who had his arm amputated to stop the progress of cancer in the absence of injections which doctors say are not available.

Iraqi doctors speak of a dramatic jump in cancer cases, genetic deformities and abnormalities in children born after 1991, blaming the use of depleted uranium munitions by U.S. and British troops as they drove Iraqi forces out of Kuwait.

The charges have been steadfastly denied in the West, which maintains there is no proven link. One U.S. health official said, "No human cancer of any type has ever been seen as a result of exposure to natural or depleted uranium."

Whatever their feelings about President Saddam Hussein, those Iraqis who spoke to me had nothing but anger for the U.S. administration and dismissed the argument of President George W. Bush that Washington's policy aimed to liberate them.

"May God enlighten him. He has no business with us. Why does he want to hit us? What does he want from us?" said an elderly woman in the Baghdad market. "Obviously he has greedy ambitions in Iraq because our soil has gold." She meant, of course, oil.

Amid the bustle of the city, one face is missing: His portrait is everywhere, but of Saddam himself there is no sign. The United States says that if Saddam spent less on his monumental palaces and on the military, there would be food and medicine enough for the people of Iraq. Driving past the brightly lit palaces, though, one wonders if Saddam ever lives in them. No one knows where the Iraqi leader is or where he sleeps.

The only regular sign that Saddam is well and in total control comes from Iraqi television, which frequently shows him in a smart suit, looking solemnly down a table at his commanders and ministers, or receiving the few dignitaries who visit Iraq nowadays.

None of the diplomats based in Baghdad has seen Saddam in person. They present their credentials to his top aide, Izzat Ibrahim, who also represents the president at official ceremonies, even his own birthday. Before the Gulf War, Saddam would often venture out to mingle with ordinary Iraqis. He no longer does so. Saddam is widely believed to use look-alikes to confuse potential assassins. He keeps ministers and commanders guessing where the next meeting will be until the last moment.

If it comes to an all-out war, diplomats in Baghdad do not expect Saddam to cede power or surrender. They say any U.S. invasion could prove more bloody than America's war against Osama bin Laden and his Taliban protectors in Afghanistan.

"True, Baghdad does not have mountains, but it is a densely populated city that presents a different order of difficulty," one envoy said. "The president prepared his bunkers long ago."

Iraq, regional commander Army General Tommy Franks, were transferring temporarily to a newly extended base in Qatar. The U.S. Air Force has a command center at Prince Sultan Air Base in Saudi Arabia, but Saudi leaders had been extremely reluctant to have their country used for any new action against Iraq.

What Sort of War?

Gulf War Two would be far different than Gulf War One. The aim the first time was to drive Saddam's forces out of Kuwait, destroying as much of his army as possible. This time the target would be Saddam himself. The United States may want to spare large parts of the Iraqi army, which could help maintain stability after the war, while targeting Saddam's elite forces of the Republican Guard. The Iraqi leader would know the moment hostilities started that his own survival was the issue. This would make him likely to show no restraint with any weapons at his disposal, or with any already-planned nonconventional attacks on U.S. targets elsewhere in the world.

United States smart weapons have become much smarter since the Gulf War, showing rapid improvement in the Kosovo operation and then the Afghan raids. The United States has developed bombs that can bore deep into the earth to attack bunkers. It has bombs that are guided by global positioning system satellites and are no longer affected by weather or smoke from burning oil fields, as the laser-guided munitions were in 1991. These new "joint direct-attack munitions" can be dropped from 35,000 feet, above much enemy fire. Apart from more accurately destroying enemy targets, the bombs are meant to minimize civilian casualties, which could be a key element in averting a hostile reaction from other Arab countries.

However much more accurate the bombs, and thus more localized the destruction, Defense Secretary Rumsfeld and U.S. military leaders concede that in any war some civilians will get killed. Given the level of anger among Arabs toward America, particularly because of the perception of a bias toward Israel and a disregard of the Palestinian cause, this is a serious issue for Washington. The possibility of popular anger rebounding on the leadership in some close U.S. allies, like Egypt, Jordan and Saudi Arabia, is clear, as well as the encouragement this would give for more violent attacks on the United States. Yet, although this cannot be discounted, some experts in Washington believe fears of a violent backlash from the "Arab street" may be exaggerated.

Some believe a tough stand by the United States may actually help restore respect for Washington, even if it does not encourage affection. By this argument, anti-American sentiment has often been whipped up by Arab governments as a distraction from their own internal problems and would be muted if television pictures showed Iraqis dancing in the streets to celebrate Saddam's departure, as Washington hopes.

Barry Rubin, Editor of the *Middle East Review of International Affairs*, argued in an essay in the U.S. publication *Foreign Affairs* in November 2002 that it was in fact the weakness of the U.S. response to guerrilla attacks in the 1990s that encouraged more attacks, not American bullying.

"Even if the United States were to pressure Israel, end sanctions on Iraq, or pull its troops out of the Persian Gulf, Arab journalists will not start praising America as a wonderful friend and noble example," he said. "Instead, further concessions will only encourage even more contempt for the United States and make the anti-American campaign more attractive."

The belief that the United States has itself partly encouraged the rash of attacks, including the bombing of U.S. embassies in Kenya and Tanzania in 1998 and of the *USS Cole* in Yemen in 2000, by projecting too weak an image in the region appears to be driving the robust approach by many in the current Bush administration. Discussing the lukewarm and, in some cases, openly hostile international reaction to the U.S. anti-Saddam crusade, Deputy Defense Secretary Wolfowitz told a Washington conference on October 16, 2002: "American resolve and determination to act—not to be hamstrung by the waverings of the weak or of those who still seek favors from the Baghdad regime— is important to embolden others to join us."

An Israeli army reservist demonstrates how to use a gas mask at a distribution center in Jerusalem, December 17, 1998.
REUTERS

If Saddam Goes, What Next?

However the war is planned, the U.S. objective is not just the overthrow of Saddam. It is primarily to create conditions for eliminating the country's alleged biological, chemical and nuclear weapons programs and lay the ground for economic recovery as well as a new, democratic system while ensuring that Iraq does not splinter or collapse into chaos.

"Our intent is not conquest or occupation of Iraq. But we will do what needs to be done to achieve the disarmament mission and to get Iraq ready for a democratic transition and then through democracy over time," said Khalilzad, of Bush's National Security Council. He told a meeting of Middle East policy experts at the Washington Institute for Near East Policy on October 5, 2002: "Iraq is a key element in a long-term strategy for the transformation of this region as a whole."

Wolfowitz echoed the hope for a wider impact from ousting Saddam. "His demise will open opportunities for governments and institutions to emerge in the Muslim world that are respectful of fundamental human dignity and freedom and that abhor the killing of innocents as an instrument of policy," he said in a speech in Washington.

United States leaders have said they will be committed to post-Saddam reconstruction, should they oust him, although many American and foreign analysts are skeptical, having seen the inclination of the Bush administration to draw down its forces in the Balkans and the limited American contribution to building up a devastated Afghanistan. Awareness of the need for rebuilding will have an impact on the shape of the war.

For example, the Pentagon may use devices for shorting out electrical power plants rather than simply blow them up. Where possible, they may avoid smashing bridges and rail networks, using more precision bombing or stealthy special forces attacks, kicking out the legs of Saddam's power base by hitting his own guards, his homes and his weapons stocks.

Despite the risk of further inflaming Arab opinion, as well as Iraqi nationalism, such an ambitious assault could well involve installation of an American-headed transition administration, the kind of mechanism employed in Japan after World War Two. Proponents of this approach say some strong central power will be needed to work on destroying weapons of mass destruction, purging the military and political leaders, managing oil production and overseeing the civilian bureaucracy. Washington realizes the importance of this being a coalition operation to counter suggestions of American imperial intentions and ensure America alone will not have to commit the forces and expertise as well as foot the bill for the huge Iraq reconstruction program.

The Bush administration has considered working to create a government in exile in advance, but no obviously strong candidates have appeared. Taking this step could alienate potential military defectors inside Iraq who may believe they deserve a role in power. Khalilzad said it was likely that "there would have to be liberation first, and then a government put in place, or put together of the Iraqis."

If Bush finally opts to invade there will be a handful of key questions:

What Will Happen to Saddam?

Experience with the elusive Osama bin Laden and the Taliban's Mullah Omar has shown that driving someone from power does not mean getting them in custody. Should Saddam be found alive, there will be strong pressure for him to be tried for war crimes. The Bush administration has been preparing the ground for this, gathering legal evidence itself and giving financial backing to other organizations trying to build up cases against Iraqi leaders.

Apart from Saddam himself, leading figures likely to be targeted would be his two sons, Uday and Qusay, as well the vice president of the Revolutionary Command Council, Izzat Ibrahim, and Ali Hassan al-Majeed, nicknamed "Chemical Ali." He led the "Anfal" repression of the Kurds in the late 1980s that included gassing thousands of civilians.

The form such trials may take was unclear, although there has been speculation that they might be held in a post-Saddam Iraq staffed

American Patriot missile batteries positioned near the Israeli city of Tel Aviv, December 18, 1998. Patriot missiles were used to intercept Iraqi Scud missiles in the 1991 Gulf War. REUTERS

in part by international jurists. Defense Secretary Rumsfeld has mused publicly over the possibility of Saddam finding a foreign exile.

What Will Happen to Iraq?

The number one priority for the United States as well as many other regional states will be to maintain Iraq's present makeup and not allow it to break into three—the Kurdish-run north, the Sunni-dominated

An Iraqi man waves a sword during celebrations of Saddam Hussein's 65th birthday in Tikrit, the Iraqi leader's hometown, April 28, 2002. REUTERS

middle and the Shi'ite south. Turkey fears creation of an eventual Kurdish state that would tempt its own Kurdish minority to resume their rebellion, and other regional powers insist Iraq's territorial integrity must be secured.

It will be vital that the various factions feel assured of getting a fair share of the revenues from oil, which is spread across the country. Massive foreign aid, and action by international agencies, will be needed to rebuild a country whose development was stunted by the Iran–Iraq War, the aerial destruction of the Gulf War and the deprivations of economic sanctions since then. Iraq's scores of billions of dollars of foreign debt, as well as billions of dollars it is obliged to pay Kuwait in damages for the Gulf War, will have to be assessed and dealt with, putting a big burden on the emerging state.

Experience of American commitment to follow up on military intervention with effective help in creating functioning democratic institutions has not been encouraging. Apart from the disastrous Somali adventure, many point to a festering sore closer to home—Haiti, where the United States intervened to oust a military leader in 1994 but allowed the country to lapse again into hopeless near-anarchy. There will be powerful calls on Iraq's oil, including those from Russia, which is determined to get billions of dollars of Iraqi debt repaid and to reap some reward from its investments over the decades.

What Will Happen to the War Against Terrorism?

One great U.S. fear of launching an invasion of Iraq at this time, when the United States is engaged with its allies around the world on rooting out highly elusive terrorism networks, is that it will encourage more people to join that network. General Wesley Clark, the former NATO commander, said in a commentary in *Time* magazine in October that it was essential "to have a post-conflict plan in place to assure that the consequences of our actions do not supercharge the al Qaeda recruiting machine." Bush has said action against Iraq is part of the war against terrorism. If intervention against Iraq now closes down one potential source of biological, chemical and possibly nuclear weapons

IRAQ ATTACK OPTIONS

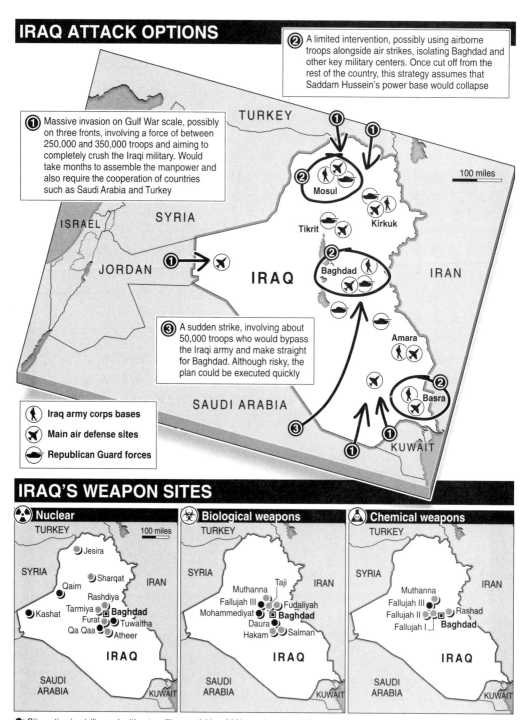

② A limited intervention, possibly using airborne troops alongside air strikes, isolating Baghdad and other key military centers. Once cut off from the rest of the country, this strategy assumes that Saddam Hussein's power base would collapse

① Massive invasion on Gulf War scale, possibly on three fronts, involving a force of between 250,000 and 350,000 troops and aiming to completely crush the Iraqi military. Would take months to assemble the manpower and also require the cooperation of countries such as Saudi Arabia and Turkey

③ A sudden strike, involving about 50,000 troops who would bypass the Iraqi army and make straight for Baghdad. Although risky, the plan could be executed quickly

100 miles

TURKEY

SYRIA

ISRAEL

JORDAN

IRAQ

IRAN

SAUDI ARABIA

KUWAIT

Mosul   Kirkuk   Tikrit   Baghdad   Amara   Basra

(👤) Iraq army corps bases

(✈) Main air defense sites

(⬅) Republican Guard forces

IRAQ'S WEAPON SITES

☢ Nuclear

100 miles

TURKEY
SYRIA
IRAN
IRAQ
SAUDI ARABIA
KUWAIT

Jesira
Sharqat
Qaim
Rashdiya
Kashat   Tarmiya   Baghdad
Furat   Tuwaitha
Qa Qaa   Atheer

☣ Biological weapons

TURKEY
SYRIA
IRAN
IRAQ
SAUDI ARABIA
KUWAIT

Taji
Muthanna
Fallujah III   Fudaliyah
Mohammediyat   Baghdad
Daura
Hakam   Salman

☠ Chemical weapons

TURKEY
SYRIA
IRAN
IRAQ
SAUDI ARABIA
KUWAIT

Muthanna
Fallujah III
Fallujah II   Rashad
Fallujah I   Baghdad

● Site active in civilian or legitimate military activities (U.N. monitored until December 1998)

◖ Destroyed or inactive site (1991–1998)

Sources: International Institute of Strategic Studies; GlobalSecurity.org

for a terrorist group hoping to attack the United States, that will be a victory, the administration says.

What Will Happen to Oil?

The interruption of Iraqi oil production by war would have little impact on world supplies, experts believe. Although prices would be driven up, at least initially, experience of the first Gulf War suggests they would quickly come back down unless the conflict widened to include other big oil producers in the Gulf or threatened to further inflame Arab–Israeli hostilities. The current world economic slowdown has helped by reducing demand for oil. Over the medium term prices would probably fall as Iraq's oil production recovered and more and more Iraqi oil reached the world market. In 2002, Iraq was producing less than 2 million barrels per day, about 3 percent of world production. This was down from a peak of 3.5 million, a level which experts say could be restored within a few years.

Many countries fear that the United States will take control of Iraq's reserves, estimated at more than 110 billion barrels and second only to those of Saudi Arabia. Russia has massive investments it wants to see turn a profit, as does France. At the same time, Russia has an interest in limiting Iraq's future oil production to avert a steep decline in world prices that would shrink revenue from its own oil. These states and others with a big stake in the future of Iraqi oil, including China and Saudi Arabia itself, have been torn between opposing U.S. aggression against Saddam and maintaining good ties with Washington to ensure their interests will not be blocked should the United States invade.

What Will Happen to Israel?

As in the Gulf War, Saddam is certain to try to draw in Israel, perhaps by repeating his Scud missile attacks of the Gulf War. If he could induce Israel to retaliate, this would make it hard for other Arab countries to continue cooperating with the U.S.-led war. It is conventional wisdom in Israel that by not responding to the 39 Scud missile attacks in 1991, Israel's deterrence in the Arab world was undermined. Prime Minister Ariel Sharon has said his country reserves the right to respond whenever it is attacked, but Bush urged restraint and promised to do all he could to stop any Iraqi attacks. The situation would become more complicated if there were an upsurge of suicide attacks inside Israel or if Syrian-backed guerrillas should intervene.

How Far Will America Go?

There has never been any question that the United States' vastly superior military would defeat Saddam. More debatable was the impact this would have on the region and on the Middle East peace process and whether the United States would be able to draw sufficient support and show enough commitment to reconstruct Iraq politically and economically. To repeat the experience of a country like Haiti, the object of past U.S. intervention and subsequent neglect, would be far more dangerous with a state as big and as crucially placed as Iraq.

But the U.S. face-off with Iraq, and the way Washington has dealt with friends, enemies and other big powers in the crisis, has illuminated a radical shift in the sole superpower's view of its place in the world since the end of the Cold War, a shift that could influence global development for decades.

The September 11 attacks, which made Americans suddenly aware of the deep hatred some abroad have for their country and of their own vulnerability, coincided with the rise in Washington of leaders who had long argued for a more aggressive national stance, particularly against what they considered "rogue" states like Iraq.

They were impatient with the limitations of working within multinational organizations and alliances.

Even before he came to power in January 2001, Bush had shown a new willingness to act unilaterally, to renounce treaties and international obligations he did not believe were in America's interests. The watchwords of post-World War Two national security policy—containment and deterrence—were joined by another concept that stirred fear and resentment in allies and enemies—pre-emptive and even preventive force. This seemed to challenge United Nations concepts of self-defense and national sovereignty. Rather than work through existing international organizations, U.S. initiatives like that against Iraq could be carried out by what Bush's national security adviser Condoleezza Rice called "coalitions of the willing."

In a speech at the U.S. Military Academy at West Point on June 1, 2002, Bush said that America would "defend the peace against the threats from terrorists and tyrants" and that the U.S. military was being transformed so it "is ready to strike at a moment's notice in any dark corner of the world." The president called on Americans "to be ready for pre-emptive action, when necessary, to defend our liberty and to defend our lives."

The revised national security strategy issued in the fall of 2002 formalized the new approach. "Given the goals of rogue states and terrorists, the United States can no longer solely rely on a reactive posture as we have in the past. The inability to deter a potential attacker, the immediacy of today's threats and the magnitude of potential harms that could be caused by our adversaries' choice of weapons do not permit that option. We cannot let our enemies strike first," it said.

John Ikenberry, professor of Geopolitics and Global Justice at Washington's Georgetown University, wrote that the Bush administration was preparing to "use its unrivalled military power to manage global order." In an article in the November 2002 issue of the journal *Foreign Affairs*, he wrote: "The United States appears to be degrading the rules and institutions of the international community, not enhancing them. To the rest of the world, neo-imperial thinking has more to do with exercising power than with exercising leadership."

It was the deep misgivings of other world leaders about the new U.S. policy, seen as a refusal to compromise with the positions of others and insistence on the pre-eminence of American interests, that lay behind the weeks of wrangling at the United Nations before the Security Council unanimously passed a resolution on November 8, 2002. It backed the main elements of the tough U.S. position on Iraq, holding out a warning of "serious consequences" if Saddam did not comply with demands to allow in U.N. weapons inspectors and to disarm. During the debates, Bush's gung-ho approach to ousting Saddam ran up against more cautious positions from France, China, Russia, Germany and most other states.

French President Jacques Chirac, who carried the banner for opposition to the U.S.-led rush to act against Iraq, said at a meeting of

French-speaking countries in Beirut on October 18, 2002: "In the modern world the use of force should only be a last and exceptional resort. It should only be allowed in the case of legitimate defense, or by a decision by the competent international bodies. Whether we are talking about making Iraq adhere to its obligations, relaunching the Israeli–Palestinian peace process or resolving conflicts in Africa, the same logic of legitimacy has to inspire all of us, because only this firmly guards us against temptations of adventure."

For Bush, disarming Iraq is not an adventure. For him inaction, not action, is the riskier choice. "To assume this regime's good faith is to bet the lives of millions and the peace of the world in a reckless gamble," he told the world in his September 12, 2002, speech to the United Nations General Assembly.

The United States is quite capable of showing that by using its unparalleled economic and military strength it can oust what it sees as a brutal and threatening ruler half a world away. But the world will be watching how it chooses to do so, with or without international endorsement.

Writers

Bernd Debusmann

has reported from more than 100 countries. He worked seven years in the Middle East, based in Cairo and Beirut. He was shot twice on assignment, covering a battle in Beirut and in an assassination attempt prompted by his reports on Syrian dissident crackdowns. He covered the Iran–Iraq and Gulf Wars. Debusmann is Reuters News Editor for the Americas.

Paul Holmes

was Bureau Chief in Jerusalem from 1997 to 2000. He has reported from some 40 countries, including from both sides during the Gulf War. He is Reuters Editor, Political and General News, and lives in New York.

Evelyn Leopold

is Reuters United Nations Bureau Chief and has covered every twist and turn of U.N. weapons inspections and the resolutions on Iraq.

Alistair Lyon

is Reuters Middle East Diplomatic Correspondent. After a recent trip to Tehran, he gives a unique insight into how Iraq's powerful neighbor, Iran, views the crisis.

Samia Nakhoul

has covered civil wars, hijackings, hostage crises, political assassinations and the Gulf War during a long career in Middle East journalism. In 1991, she began reporting on the Egyptian Islamist insurgency, returning to Beirut as Bureau Chief, Lebanon and Syria, in 2001. She is a Lebanese citizen.

David Storey

is an expert in U.S. national security affairs and is based in Washington, D.C. He has worked as a foreign correspondent for Reuters in London, Bonn, Vienna, Warsaw, Bangkok, Ankara, Harare and Nairobi.

Mark Trevelyan

has reported from five continents and 25 countries since 1986. Based in London, he is Reuters Deputy News Editor for Europe, the Middle East and Africa.

Patrick Worsnip

has worked as the Reuters State Department Correspondent and is an expert in Middle East and foreign affairs. Worsnip wrote a series of striking eyewitness accounts after Saddam used chemical weapons on the inhabitants of the Kurdish town of Halabja in 1988.

Photographers

Havakuk Levison, *page 167*

Jerry Lampen, *pages 149, 168*

Peter Macdiarmid, *page 152*

Win McNamee, *page 36*

Stephanie McGehee, *page 146*

Patrick de Noirmont, *page 78*

Charles Platiau, *page 104*

Damir Sagolj, *pages 64, 72, 111, 159*

Jamal Saidi, *page 15*

Suhaib Salem, *page 69*

Ira Schwarz, *page 81*

David Silverman, *page 164*

Shannon Stapleton, *page 157*

Mike Theiler, *page 150*

Philippe Wojazer, *pages 105, 106*